An Elephant Called
Malla Prasad

AF553542

An Elephant Called
Malla Prasad

Ashok Singh

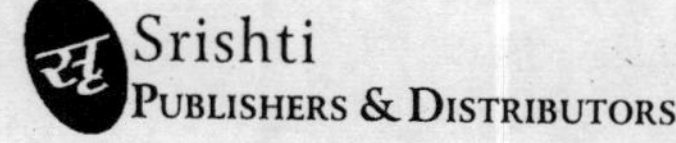

Srishti
Publishers & Distributors

SRISHTI PUBLISHERS & DISTRIBUTORS
64-A, Adhchini
Sri Aurobindo Marg
New Delhi 110 017

Copyright © Ashok Singh 2000

Copyright © SRISHṬI PUBLISHERS & DISTRIBUTORS 2000
First published in 2000 by Srishti Publishers & Distributors

ISBN 81-87075-58-9
Rs. 95.00

Cover Design, Photography and Typeset by
Arrt Creations
45 Nehru Apartment, Kalkaji, New Delhi 110 019
e-mail: arrt@vsnl.com

Printed and bound in India by
Saurabh Print-O-Pack, Noida

All rights reserved. No part of this publication may
be reproduced, stored in a retrieval system, or transmitted,
in any form or by any means, electronic, mechanical,
photocopying, recording, or other wise,
without the prior written permission of the Publisher.

Dedication

I pay special thanks to my parents
who lives in an extremely rural atmosphere,
gave me the best possible education
due to which I am able to
write this book.

Contents

THE SONEPUR FAIR

"Why are you looking at me like that for?", asked the wasp. The baby elephant went on concentrating at the little yellow creature that was buzzing before it.

"Come on, tell me what are you upto?".

The elephants head turned to the left and the trunk shot up sending the wasp flying headlong into a tree trunk. It hit its head on the bark and tumbled down in a daze.

"Now why did you have to do that for?".

"I am swatting wasps".

"I hit my head on the tree trunk, it aches".

"Serves you right for being a pest, your buzzing irritates me".

The wasp gathered itself and regaining its buzzing it flew to a height three feet above the baby elephant.

"Shoo off", squealed the little pachyderm".

"Why?".

"Your buzzing irritates me".

"I won't, anyway, I feel sorry for you".

"Why?".

"You 're a slave".

"A slave?".

"Yes, a slave, to be bought and sold for".

"Whose going to buy and sell me?".

"The humans you dope. Ask the elephant next to you, and the ones further down the line. They will tell you that you are all slaves of the humans and not a free citizen like me".

The baby elephant swung its trunk sending the tip as high as possible in an attempt to re-hit the wasp. The latter had however sensed the attack and buzzed itself a foot higher, out of reach of the trunk. "You won't get me again", it said.

"Look at your size and mine", replied the elephant, "you will realize who I am, and who you are".

"That's the irony of it", continued the wasp. "I am tiny, but a free citizen. You are huge and strong, but a slave".

The little pachyderm turned to the elephant next to him. It was a huge male tusker. "Uncle, this wasp says that we are slaves and he himself is a free citizen", he asked. "It it True?"

"True son", replied the tusker. "We are slaves, though we are big and strong. And the irony of it is the little wasp is really a free citizen".

The baby elephant turned to face the tiny creature who had buzzed down a feet only to buzz up again as the little trunk swung and missed it once more".

"Don't try that again", teased the wasp. "I'm too smart for that now".

"Okay free citizen, Where are we just now?".

"At the Sonepur fair you dope. You have been brought here all the way from Assam, from Kaziranga I get it. You had been poached".

"What's poached? I remember I fell into a ditch, and some humans hauled me out and brought me here in a truck. At least they called it a truck. I enjoyed the ride with the countryside rushing past me".

"That is what they call poaching. The hunters either kill you or catch you to be sold, that's why you are tied to the tree".

"Okay, wise guy what else do you see here?.

"Plenty. You aren't the only animals for sale. There are camels, cats, dogs, mice, snakes, horses, cows, donkeys, deer and different types of birds".

"That means they are all slaves?".

"Yes they are all slaves, to be bought and sold at the humans will, and to toil for them. .You see they aren't free creatures like us wasps".

The baby elephant wondered. It was too little and inexperienced to realize that it was in the Sonepur fair. The fair was regarded as the biggest in Asia and its speciality was the buying and selling of animals and birds. Merchants from all over India came with their wares to sell them here.

The fair took place in the month of October over an area approximating six thousand acres of Mango grove with one thousand acres reserved for the residential section, fifteen hundred acres for the market section, fifteen hundred acres for the entertainment section and two thousand acres for the animal section.

The market and entertainment section was situated on open treeless ground with rows of shops selling their wares from cheap trinkets to decorate women's noses and ears to expensive perfumes and sarees, to beautify them. The fair was generally a rural affair so you had huge makeshift showroom's advertising agricultural machinery from harvesters to tractor's and jeeps. The entertainment section was of course an ear splitting affair with giant wheels, hurdy gurdies, and rows of theatres advertising gaudily dressed, gauche looking dancing girls through extremely loud loudspeakers which could easily bust the ear drum's if played a little louder. The humans loved the different games, the giant wheels and hurdy gurdies, and the free citizens, the little wasps frequented this area because of the abundance of sweet shops. They loved hovering and buzzing over the white round rosogullas, the chocolate brown gulab jamun's, and the yellow laddooes. They of course passed on germs which resulted in the human's who ate these delicacies getting diarrhea or some other stomach related illness.

The residential and animal section were in a Mango grove. The poor villagers slept on bedsheets laid out under Mango trees while the richer people were allotted five thousand square feet of tarpaulin boundary walled land to pitch their tents and reside in. A ditch was dug and covered with planks with a round hole in the middle. This was a make shift latrine, and the planks would be removed and the ditch would be filled with mud when the fair was wound up.

The animal section where the little elephant was tied to a mango tree was the main attraction. People from all over India came to buy and sell cats, dogs, mice, rabbits, chicken, deer, goats, camels, cows, bulls, horses, elephants and donkeys. Plots of land were cordoned off to house the animals with a section exclusively for the birds like peacocks, mynah's, different types of parrots, budgriga's and quail.

"There's a human coming this way", exclaimed the wasp.

"Where?".

"There".

The baby elephant was soon looking at a weird looking specimen of the human race who was now standing directly before him. The person was chocolaty brown in complexion, tall, bald, and had a longish face with huge greyish whiskers under the nose which seemed to flow upwards to the ears. There was some white hair around the bald pate, and a billy goats beard hung from the chin. The fellow was wearing a black kurta over a black lungi which was wrapped around his naval under a huge paunch. Over his shoulder hung a double barrel shotgun with a belt over his chest which was studded with red cartridges.

"Yikes, he looks like a poacher to me", confessed the wasp.

"Look at him, he's staring at me", exclaimed the elephant. "I feel like giving him a thwack with my trunk".

"Hey, hey, hey, control it, he's got a gun over his shoulder".

"So what's with a gun?".

"Its a fire stick, and if used, it could fill your head with hot round balls. You would be dead in a jiffy."

The man was now twirling his moustache as he surveyed the elephant.

"Now why is he doing that for?", asked the baby elephant.

"He's in deep thought", replied the wasp.

The man walked around to the left of the elephant. Being suspicious, the little pachyderm turned to face him.

"Good", said the man. "I think my master will like this animal".

"What did he say?", asked the baby elephant looking aside.

"He says he likes you", replied the wasp. "I think you will soon be his slave. I think he is a mahout".

"What's a mahout", asked the elephant.

"Oh its an elephant trainer. A person who beats elephants and makes them obedient".

The man spoke in hindi and threw a garland of flowers over the elephants head as a sign that he was interested in the animal. "Where is the middle man", he shouted. "The master will be proud. He will say, Jehangir Khan always has the right choice, and he will give me a reward".

A thin looking person who had tied the baby elephant to the tree walked up greeting the questioner with a "Namastay", and "yes what do you want?". He was wearing a white kurta over a white dhoti.

"How much you want for this elephant?", asked the moustached man.

"This beautiful elephant".

"Yes".

"Twelve thousand rupees".

"Its too expensive".

"Its cheap".

"I'll leave the haggling to the master".

"Okay call him, I will be waiting for you".

The man called Jehangir Khan turned around and walked off with his right hand holding the gun butt so that it did not sway with the gait of his walk. He took long strides as he walked past the rows of elephants, camels, cows, and other animals, towards the residential complex where he passed rows of gaudily coloured tarpaulins boundary walls to the square piece of land that had been allotted to his master. The latter was sitting on a cot in the shade of a tree.

In the middle of the plot there were two tents, one

for the master and the other for the attendants. In the north eastern corner were parked two jeeps and the makeshift latrines were to the south of the tents with a hand pump near them. Wood had been piled near a makeshift kitchen.

Jehangir Khan salaamed the master as he approached. His torso bent down low as his right hand swung up and down as he uttered the words "Salaam Alaikum".

"So Jehangir what is it?", the master asked. He was a portly looking gentleman and was fair in complexion, tall, and was wearing a vest over an expensive dhoti. He had a gold chain around his neck and his finger's were studded with diamond rings. His face was round and chubby with hanging jowls pudgy lips and a short chin. He was Avadesh Prasad Singh the zemindar of Ramnagar and was of the Bhumihar caste, a ruling land owning caste of Bihar. "Yes what is it?", he asked.

"Sahib I have seen a baby elephant. I think it will be perfect for the master."

"Okay, we will see it later."

"No sir, we should not delay."

"Why?"

"Because it is a baby male and the price is reasonable and some one else may buy it."

"How much is the price?"

"Twelve thousand has been demanded."

"Can it be reduced?"

"Yes, at the most two thousand."

The zemindar said a "very good," and lifted his huge body into a standing position. He had a huge bottom which seemed to peep through the thin fabric of his expensive dhoti, and soon he and his peeping bottom disappeared into the tent and re-emerged wearing a silk kurta, and the baby elephant was confronted with two specimens of the human race admiringly looking at him.

"Now what do these two want?", asked the elephant.

"The mahout has returned with his master", replied the wasp.

The zemindar looked approvingly at the little pachyderm as he stood holding an end of his dhoti in one hand. "I like it Jehangir, I like it", he said," where is the middleman."

"Yes sahib?"

"How much do you want for it?"

"Twelve thousand sahib."

"I will give you nine thousand."

The deal was clinched at ten thousand, the money paid, the rope tied to the tree was untied, and Jehangir led the little elephant to the zamindar's residence where stakes were driven into the ground and the elephants legs were tied to them.

A couple of days passed while the zemindar and his attendants roamed the fair haggling with the shopkeepers. The evenings were alive with garishly made up dancing girls who danced mujrahs and entertained the landlord in a closed tent. A couple of "chaat", eating day's more and two camels were bought. The zemindar wanted to continue enjoying the dancing girls and since it was expensive feeding the animals in the fair, Jehangir Khan was ordered to take his three wards back to the village where the food items were available free. The baby elephant soon found itself walking behind the two camels with Jehangir Khan perched on the male one's hump.

"Where are we going?" asked the baby elephant.

"Don't know," replied the female camel. "Well just have to walk behind our male friend here and go to where ever that man with a billy goats beard, takes us to."

"Back in the fair there was a wasp who told me that we were slaves of these humans. Is it true.?"

"One hundred percent true. Don't you see how he sits contemptuously on the gentle camels hump. His proud face and the twirling of his moustache says so."

The baby elephant stayed quiet and the three quietly followed the man with the huge whiskers and a billy goats beard to wherever he took them, to Ramnagar and zemindar Avadesh Prasad's mansion where the three animals got a fright. The entrance of the zamindar's compound was guarded by two huge lions who sat on their haunches on both sides of the gate with outstretched paws and mouth wide open showing canine teeth.

"Yeeek's those are lions," belched the female camel.

"I'm getting out of here," squealed the little elephant as it shot off across the fields in a run.

"Stop," yelled Jehangir, "stop, Jogi, come out."

"What is it?", shouted a man from behind the lions.

"The elephant has run away, help me."

Jehangir turned his camel around who extra willingly did so. It also wanted to scamper off, but was being held back by Jehangir's tight grip on the reigns. The pachyderm was now a little spot running through the wheat fields, so Jehangir let go off the reigns and gave the camel a swat on the rump. "Run after the elephant," he yelled, "Well have to catch him".

The camel raced off after the elephant into the wheat fields just as a black horse galloped out of the gates with a short bare backed cowherd sitting astride it. "When ever the master buys a new animal", grumbled the horse, "the silly creature gets spooked by those idiotic looking cement lions, and I have to chase them and bring them back".

"Wait, stop", belched the male camel at the elephant as it ran its jaunty run closely followed by the female camel who was now galloping. Soon the black horse was alongside the camels and was galloping for all it was worth, as it winnied to the elephant to stop.

The baby elephant did finally stop, but not until it reached the tarmaced road which led back to Sonepur and the fair.

The horse galloped upto the pachyderm as the camels drew up. "Those lions are man made you dopes", scolded the stallion. "They are lifeless statues made of cement and stone chips."

"Are you sure they are lifeless?", grunted the female camel. "My god, I got the fright of my life."

"Me too", squealed the little elephant, "that's why I ran away."

"Now cool yourselves", ordered the horse as it slowly closed in onto the elephant. "Those two lions are as immovable as that tree over there. They are just decoration pieces for the masters entrance gate."

The cowherd jumped off the horse and ran and caught the rope tied around the baby elephant's neck.

"Cool down, don't be afraid", whinnied the horse, "he means you no harm."

Jehangir Khan had also jumped down from his perch on the male camels hump and was holding the other side of the rope, and catching hold of the ear he led the elephant back towards the double lioned gate. "Jogi", he ordered, "take the camels and the horse back. I'll take care of the elephant."

Jogi the cowherd was a short dark boy, bare backed with only a little soiled loin cloth tied around his naval. His head was hidden under a dirty turban, and he smelt of cow. Taking hold of the camel's and horse's reign's he led them back towards the double lioned gate, as he himself walked directly behind the pachyderm prodding it whenever it resisted Jehangir Khan.

Soon the two humans and scared animals were through the gates and inside the zamindar's compound. The compound was square in shape and covered an area of three acres. In front of the animals was a double storied white building with a verandah in the front. The animals themselves were standing on ground which should have been an exotic garden. To the left was a little private temple and the boundary wall which ran all around the campus, and to the right was a hedge beyond which was a long cowshed made of mud walls and a low thatched roof. It was towards this cowshed that the animals were led.

The three creatures soon found themselves in front of the cowshed which faced the eastern wall of the mansion. Before them was a little field to the right of which was the boundary wall, and a tall one roomed structure. It was made of brick walls and was twenty feet long, twenty feet broad and twenty five feet high and was roofed with corrugated iron sheets. It was the "Haathikhana", the little elephants new home. The ground in front of the Haathikhana was flat and dusty with a little hump near the boundary wall near which a red tractor and a bullock cart stood.

"It seems this is our new home", belched the female camel.

"It does look nice", mumbled the pachyderm just before it got another fright. A host of belches and mooe's emanated from the cowshed.

"What was that?", belched the male camel, "Why the row?"

"Its those foolish cows again", neighed the horse. It was a stallion of Arabian breed. "They always behave foolishly when a newcomer arrives. They are irritated with your presence, and think you will occupy a part of their cowshed".

"Yes, yes, where are the bull's", mooed the cows "They seem to disappear just when we need them."

A cow poked its head out off the cowshed. "Push off you three", it mooed. "Piss off".

"Shoo off", another belched.

"Where are our husbands", belched a third.

"They are all tied behind the mansion", replied a short horned cow.

"Well that's one hell of a reception", belched the male camel. "How many cows are there in there."

"Seventy five", neighed the horse. "They are tied to trough's in one long row, and their husbands are tied to stakes behind the mansion."

"Will the three of you go to hell", mooed a little Jersey cow after it poked its head out of the cowshed.

"I'm coming my darling's, I'm coming", belched a bull from behind the mansion as it pulled at the rope that tied it to a wooden stake. It had heard the SOS that its darling's had mooed and was adamant to free itself and go to their aid. “I’m coming my dears, I’m coming”, it belched.

“Shut up”, shouted Jogi as he picked up a long stick and thwacked the most vociferous of the cows on their huge rumps just as the huge bull broke free and had come round the mansions corner. “This will teach you all to make a fuss”, he shouted.

Now this was not liked by the bull. Who would like the sight of his beautiful wife’s beautiful rump being thwacked by a huge stick? This was too much. It was impertinence. The cowherd had outraged the modesty of his wives. He would be taught a lesson. He had to be taught a lesson so the bull snorted and belched. “I’ll teach you, I’ll teach you to thwack the rumps of my harem”, and charged.

The cowherd saw the bull charge so he shinnied up a mango tree just before the bull rammed into the trunk. Looking up at the cowherd, it snorted. “You do that again you nincompoop and I’ll ram my horn’s into you”.

The scared cow herd looked down.

“Yah you monkey”, continued the bull. “You haven’t tasted my horns. They won’t feel nice when I ram them into your bottom, I assure you”.

“Yah go, go”, shouted the cow herd.

“I’m going you lily livered idiot. But remember the next time you slander a rump, and I’ll climb up there after you”.

The cowherd climbed down only when it saw the bull lumber off to some distance as it mumbled, “Chivalry man chivalry you should be taught how to treat the weaker sex”. However he scampered back up when the bull turned and charged.

"I missed you again you black skinned human", belched the bull, "now take this as a warning. If I catch you thwacking my wives again, I won't be kind".

The bull lumbered off, and only when it was a safe distance away did the cowherd dare come down again.

"Well that was one hell of a reception", commented the camel. "How many more bull's are there around?".

"There are eight of them", replied the stallion. "They are a huge joint family with eight bulls to seventy five cows".

"Wow", replied the camel. "What a family".

"The bull's have divided the cows amongst themselves and call their families their harem".

"What about you?", asked the female camel. "Are you single or double?".

"Double".

"Where's you're lesser half?".

"There", the stallion pointed his nose to a white mare tied to a trough in a corner of the cow shed. "Isn't she pretty?". "I don't find horses pretty", commented the male camel.

"Here's our food", replied the horse as he saw Jehangir walk over with a bundle of hay.

"My what a reception we got", mumbled the male camel. "What a reception".

"I 'm not going to eat hay", squealed the baby elephant. "I want to eat banana's or papaya's, I don't like hay".

Jehangir put down the hay and took out three wooden stakes. He hammered one into the ground in front of the female camel, and another in front of the male camel. Taking two ropes he made a noose around the camels necks and tied the other end to the stakes.

Taking the hay he spread it out equally between the two animals. Satisfied, he led the baby elephant by the ear to the "Haathikhana".

"I won't eat hay", squealed the elephant, but stopped when it saw a mass of mango leave's heaped in a corner of the hall. "Now that's what I call good food", it rumbled and rushed forward taking a trunkful into its little mouth. "This is delicious".

"That's that!", thought Jehangir. "Now to tie the elephant, have my dinner and go to sleep. I've had a tiring day today and I need a rest. Tomorrow I'll need all the strength I have to look after these three animals.

THE NEW FRIEND

It was the month of January when Bihar is at its coldest best. The Biharis hate this season, the cold climate and prefer the hot summers or damp monsoons when one can move around in a thin vest and dhoti. No one liked this ankle freezing, chest colding season called winter when you have to wear kilo's of clothes to stay warm. It was alright for the rich who wore expensive woolen's and slept in expensive blankets or fat quilts. It was the poor who suffered. Most of them could not afford the blankets or quilts and were at their wits end to ward off the cold. They had to rely on gunny sacks stuffed with hay, sewn together for a mattress and gunny sacks stuffed with hay for a quilt. In the evenings they would make little fires around which they would sit chatting into the night until the fire went out and after that God help them till the next morning.

Jehangir khan was one of the lucky few. He had to himself a whole haystack which his master owned. He and Jogi had burrowed into the hay, and made a cave each which was around seven feet deep and two feet in diameter. It was into this cave that Jehangir retired into after tying the elephant near the pile of leaves.

Laying down the gun comfortingly beside him, Jehangir was soon lost in thought. He was a lonely man and was single. He did have a family once. A wife, and two children. A boy and a girl. He had however lost them in one of those hindu muslim riots that occasionally sprouted up in the countryside of Bihar. Gangs of militant hindus had stormed his village as gangs of muslims were storming hindu villages elsewhere. The marauders had barged into his hut and shot his wife and spiked his children. He would have also died if it had not been for the zemindar who saved him. The latter had shot two of his hindu brethren who were about to kill him. That was why Jehangir was fiercely loyal to him. He owed his life to the master. The latter had provided him with the money for his families funeral. Because of his fierce loyalty to the zemindar he was on the hit list of the naxalites, and that was why the gun felt re-assuring beside him.

Jehangir himself was a poor man and sympathized with the Communists. Why should a person be so rich and own elephants, and cows, and horses and jeeps and tractors and hundreds of acres of land while others hardly owned the clothes they wore? Why should people die because they could not afford the expensive medicines and doctors? Why shouldn't humans be equal? Secretly Jehangir hoped that the communist party would be elected to power. He however did not believe in the ways and doctrine of the naxalites. They believed in a revolution, by forcibly coming to power. Killing wasn't a problem for them, and they wouldn't stop at annihilating the entire land owning class to reach their goal. This wasn't necessary since India was a democracy and had an elected government. The naxalites believed in anarchy. They forcibly took land if the landlord was weak. If he put up resistance, they didn't hesitate to kill.

Avadesh Prasad had fiercely backed the people fighting the naxalites and being his loyal servant Jehangir had also done the same. That was why he was high in their hit list. Why kill and maim. If you wanted communism, then go to the people and make them accept it, explain it to them, then get voted to power. All this killing was unnecessary.

Jehangir went to sleep and in his dreams he saw his little daughter and son sitting astride the baby elephant he had just brought back. How they loved the little pachyderm. "Get up papa the little boy said, "it is getting hot". Jehangir opened an eye and realized it was early dawn and a little sunray was peeping in.

"Get up, Jehangir", the sunray seemed to say.

"No, I won't" Jehangir mumbled. "You are too weak just now and it is cold outside. I will not get up now. I'll wait till you become stronger and warmer. Then only will I venture out".

The little ray got irritated, "What?, me weak, I'll show you". It intensified itself and pumped more heat into its system as it ventured deeper into the hay stack hole. "Now get up", it ordered.

"I won't" thought Jehangir, "you're still too weak".

This human is stubborn thought the sun ray as it intensified itself more, pumped more heat into its system and ventured deeper into the cave till the mahout felt stuffy. "Now that will bring you out".

The ray was successful because Jehangir finally slid out and rubbing his eye's he pulled out his lota and walked to the hand pump and filled it with water. Walking with the lota he walked out of the gates to the adjoining fields to defecate. After doing the needful he broke a twig from a mango tree and proceeded to chew the end into a pulp which he later used to scrub his teeth. Doing so he walked upto the Haathikhana to see what the little elephant was doing.

"Now that is not like a good boy", the mahout commented.

The baby elephant was spraying mud with its trunk on its own back.

"You behave like a street urchin", continued Jehangir, "Now I will have to give you a wash".

"Jehangir", a woman shouted as he turned around. It was the zamindar's maid servant. "The mistress will be coming to see the elephant".

Jehangir was expecting the visit. "Give me half an hour", he shouted back. "I will wash it and make it presentable."

The maid servant walked off and Jehangir led the elephant to the well where he dunked the pachyderm in buckets of water and gave it a proper scrub. The elephant liked the bath and taking a trunk full of water, it squirted the liquid onto the mahout and wet his billy goat beard and bald head.

"Now why did you do that?", said Jehangir wiping the water from his face.

"You deserve a bath too", squealed the elephant.

Jehangir went on scrubbing the elephants back as the little trunk squirted water on itself.

"I'll have to prepare you for the mistress", he spoke as he scrubbed. "she might like you and give me a fat baksheesh".

Jehangir finally stopped and looked at his handiwork. The baby elephant now looked presentable. Taking hold of the left ear, he led it back to the Haathikhana from where he sent Jogi to inform the mistress that the elephant was ready for her. Fetching a garland of yellow gulmohars from the temple, he broke one end and put it around the neck. He tied up the broken ends and waited for the mistress to come.

The baby elephant was relaxed as it swung its trunk from the left to the right. "Why is this garland around my neck?", he squealed to the camels.

"Don't know, ask the cows, they may have an answer."

"What cows?, who said cows?", said a long horned Hariyanvi bovine who had stuck her head out of the shed. "Will you two camels shut up, and stop talking about us."

"Will you shut up," neighed the mare which was tethered in a corner of the cowshed. "Those animals have-not disturbed you, neither do they have any intention of doing so. So mind your own business."

"I know, I know", mooed another Jersey cow. "I know why you are siding with those creatures. You want them to annex a corner of the shed like the two of you have done."

"Haw, haw, haw", neighed the mare, "you cows are a bunch of idiots. Look at the size of the camels, they are too tall to fit in here."

"These cows are only bothered with owning their cowshed", commented the stallion. "They have no imagination at all."

"Hmmm, the horses are right, the camels are too tall to enter the cowshed." It was a tall half breed cow that spoke. She then turned to the other cows. "Now shut up all of you. Our shed is safe. Those camels cannot enter it and the elephant has got his own house."

"Look it is the masters wife coming from the mansion's verandah, she's accompanied by the maid servant and the woman is carrying a tray", said the mare.

"Now don't tell me they are going to pray to one of the new animals", commented the stallion.

"Let's have a bet", offered the mare, "if they pray to the camels, I win, if they pray to the elephant, then you win".

"The stallion will win", mooed the cows, "the mistress will pray to the elephant. We know that. Our forefather's told our forefather's who told our forefathers who told us. The knowledge has been passed down from generation to generation that the humans pray to mice, snakes, elephants, birds and especially us cows".

"Shhhh", shushed a cow, "silence please, or the cow herd will come and thwack our rumps again. It hurt yesterday and I don't want to receive another shot".

The little elephant lifted its head and saw an extremely fat lady with a thin woman walk towards him. The lady was wearing an expensive brightly coloured red sari with a gold necklace around her neck. Her fingers were studded with gold rings, and she had diamond studded ear rings hanging from her ear lobes. Her face was round with bulging cheeks and she seemed to be waddling. A thin dark maid servant was directly behind her. The woman was in direct contrast to the mistress. Her sari looked brown and dirty and was torn in places. In her hands she held a bronze prayer tray, a corner of which was filled with round yellow ball's called laddooe's. In the northern tip of the tray was a little lamp with a little flame which occasionally threatened to go off.

"Now who is this fat person?", squealed the baby elephant.

"Shush", shushed the male camel. "Some one important is coming, the cows have fallen silent".

As the woman waddled closer, Jehangir bowed down low swaying his hand to his fore head and back to his thighs in a salaam. "Salaam Alaikum", he greeted.

"Now look at this lady walking. She waddles like a duck", thought the elephant. "Why have the cow's fallen silent?".

Waddling upto the elephant the fat mistress clapped her hands in delight. "Oh what a cute little elephant", she exclaimed. "Jehangir Khan you deserve a baksheesh for bringing his holiness".

Jehangir bowed down low and swung his hand up again in a salaam. "Thank you madam, thank you", he said.

The baby elephant looked around. He did not understand this human talk and was looking for a wasp who would translate for him. Unfortunately there wasn't any around.

"How old is he", asked the fat lady.

"Twelve months, or may be a year and a half at the most".

"Shiela pass me the tray".

The maid servant handed the mistress the prayer tray.

"What a happy occasion this is", commented the mistress. "Lord Ganesh now resides in my compound".

"Yes madam", replied the maid servant.

"You mahout hold the elephant tight".

"Yes mistress".

The lady held the tray with her left hand and dipped the right hands thumb into the red vermilion powder which was in the tray. Taking out the red thumb she held out her hand and directed the thumb at the elephants for head.

"What is she doing?", thought the elephant as it moved back suspiciously. It squinted its eyes to concentrate on the thumb. "Why is she pointing that red finger at me?"

"Hold the elephant tight", the lady ordered.

The red thumb moved forward and the baby elephant moved back. Jehangir had to heave at the rope to bring the elephant forward. The thumb made contact and travelled two inches up making a red line on the fore head.

"Aaah", exclaimed the mistress, "I have put a teeka on lord Ganesh's head".

"Now what did she do that for?", thought the elephant, "I feel like giving her a shot with my trunk".

The fat lady started twirling the tray around the elephants forehead singing "Jaya Jagadisha Hare".

"Now what is she doing?", thought the elephant.

"Jaya Jagadisha Hare".

"Will you stop it".

"Jaya Jagadisha Hare".

The elephants little eyes followed the circular route the tray was taking, making the pachyderm's eye balls travel in round circles, causing the animal to feel dizzy. The tray blurred, re-focused, blurred and re-focused again.

"Jaya Jagadisha Hare".

There were two sets of fat women twirling two trays

with two little burning lamps.

"Jaya Jagadisha Harre".

One more fat woman with a tray entered the tray twirling game.

"Jaya, Jagadisha Harre".

This was too much. There were three fat ladies twirling three trays with three burning lamps. The elephant tugged to free itself from Jehangir Khan's grasp. Unfortunately the Muslim gentleman had a tight hold on him and did not let him budge. He had known what was going to happen and had anticipated the elephants reaction. "Let me be", squealed the baby elephant.

"Oooh how wonderful", exclaimed the mistress as she clapped her hands in delight, "Lord Ganesh is speaking to me".

"Let go you idiots I feel dizzy".

Mistaking the squeal for another blessing the woman continued twirling the prayer tray.

"Now I can see four of them", squealed the elephant, "please some one help me, my head aches".

"Come on Shiela", ordered the mistress, "chant with me."

The elephant closed its eyes and turned towards the camels and reopened them. There were three sets of two camels looking at him. "Sir's what are they going to do with me? There is a flame in the tray. Will they burn me?"

"We don't know", answered the three sets of two camels. "Ask the cows. They have been living here. They should know".

The elephant turned its head towards the cowshed and saw three sets of cow sheds with three sets of seventy five horned heads and two horse heads peeping out.

"Don't worry", mooed the three sets of seventy five horned heads, "She means no harm. She is only praying to you. Don't concentrate on the tray and just close your eyes".

The elephant shut its eyes tight and tried to forget the moving tray. "These humans are weird", it thought.

"The lady is a hindu", mooed the cows, "and she thinks you are an incarnation of the elephant god, lord Ganesh".

"Me an incarnation of a god?, that's weird".

"Not surprising, they pray to us also and take our dirty dung to purify their homes. They smear it over the floor."

The elephant opened its eyes and realized that two sets of everything had disappeared, so it cocked its head sideways and avoiding the moving tray, it concentrated its gaze at the cow shed.

"Come on Shiela chant louder", goaded the mistress, "Jaya Jagadisha Hare".

"You cows are kidding", squealed the elephant. "How can these humans be so dumb as to think I am a god or something. I can't do anything other than flail my trunk. I feel like thwacking the lady on the bottom. I must say she's got a huge rump".

"Oh Shiela, it is my lucky day. His holiness is showering me with blessings", drooled the mistress.

The twirling of the tray stopped and the mistresses fat hand picked up a round yellow ball from the pile and held it out. "Here take it your holiness", she exhorted.

"Now what does she want?", grumbled the elephant, "Will she rub that round thing on my forehead also?"

"Take it", mooed the seventy five horned heads who were peeping out. "They are laddooe's and are very sweet when tasted".

"Shall I take it?", squealed the elephant.

Jehangir took the yellow ball and shoved it into the elephants mouth. It tasted nice so the ball went in deeper and the elephant started chewing and savouring the taste.

The mistress held out another yellow ball, which the elephant took with its trunk and placed it in its mouth.

"Look Shiela, his holiness took the laddoo from my hand".

"Yes madam".

Chewing the laddooes the elephant squealed. "Give me some more you fat slob".

"Oooh Shiela, he spoke to me", the mistress squealed again clapping her hands in delight.

"Pass the yellow balls, you red bottomed pumpkin".

"Oooh Shiela how wonderful. His holiness is praising me. He loves talking to me".

Jehangir and the woman called Shiela had broad grins on their faces.

"What ever it is ", mumbled the elephant, "it tastes nice".

"Madam", Jehangir interrupted, "you shouldn't be out of doors for such a long time. I think you have forgotten the naxalites. See that boundary wall there. It isn't high enough, anyone could jump over it."

"Oh yes I forgot". The madam looked visibly scared. One thing the naxalites had been successful in doing was to instill fear in the hearts of the land owing community. "I forgot about the naxalites. Anyway I feel tired, and shouldn't be standing for so long. Here Shiela take the tray and you Jehangir take the laddooes and feed them to the elephant."

The madam turned around and her rump was now facing the elephant. "What a huge bottom she has", wondered the baby elephant. "Lets see how it feels". It lifted its trunk to the right and swung it across the huge rump slapping the flesh.

"My, my", thought the elephant, "that bulge was soft."

The madam was terrified. She stood still. "What was that?", she asked Jehangir not daring to look back herself.

Jehangir hadn't seen the swing the elephant had given her so he continued. "The naxalites madam".

The madam cut him short "The naxalites?".

"Yes, madam, the naxalites could".

The baby elephant had liked the feel of the rump and gave a second swing, thwacking it on the same spot it had thwacked earlier.

The mistress was petrified. She slowly opened her mouth and took in a deep breath. The air soon rushed out forming the scream "NAXALITES".

Jehangir went for his gun. He swivelled around and swung it from his shoulder and had turned just in time to see the elephant give the third thwack.

"NAXALITES", screamed the mistress as she rushed off in a waddle. "Naxalites", she went on screaming as she reached a waddling record breaking speed and huffing and puffing she ran into the verandah and dashing in she tumbled over a couch and fell flat on the floor. “Naxalites”, she whispered as she coughed and wheezed, “it was the naxalites”.

“Haw, haw, haw’, belched the cows.

“Haw, haw, haw”, belched the camels.

“Heh, heh, heh”, neighed the horses.

“Madam you shouldn’t have run like that. “The thin Shiela had caught up with the record breaker waddler and was helping her get up. “You could have killed yourself, you seem to have forgotten your heart trouble”.

“It was the naxalites Shiela”, whispered the mistress. “It was the naxalites, they attacked me”.

“It wasn’t the naxalites madam, “Shiela was suppressing her laugh. She wanted to blow up. “It was the elephant that hit you madam”.

“What?, it was the elephant?”, the mistress’s face turned from petrified to embarrassment. She sat up. “You mean to say the elephant hit me, and it wasn’t the naxalites?”

“Yes madam”.

“Ooooh how cute, its so playful Shiela.”

“Yes madam”.

Back in the Haathikhana Jehangir was rolling in laughter. In the cowshed Jogi was rolling in laughter while the animals “Haw hawed”, and “heh hehe’d”, out their guts. Jehangir Khan controlled his laugh and got up and with a serious face he walked upto the verandah and the mistress. “Madam you forgot to name the elephant. It should have a name and I would like you to give him one”.

The embarrassed mistress picked herself up and sat on the couch trying to regain as much of her composure as was possible. She wanted to be alone and wanted to get rid of the mahout. “He has a beautiful garland around his neck so call him Malla Prasad”, she suggested.

“And the camels madam?”.

“Ugh, they look ugly”, the mistress had wrinkled up her nose. “You or the villagers can name them. NOW GO.”

Jehangir turned and with a smile on his face he walked back to the chorus of “haw haws”, and “hee hee’s”. Opening the camels tether, he led them to the well where he proceeded to dunk buckets of water over them and scrub them after which he led them back to their stakes. He realized that a crowd had gathered around the baby elephant and seeing him and the camels, they surrounded the two animals.

“So Jehangir, I see you have got three more guests”, commented an elderly villager.

Jehangir did not reply but walked off to fetch some hay for the camels. Word had spread around the village about the three new animals, and the villager’s were trickling in to see for themselves. It was a dull, sleepy little village and soon there was a crowd surrounding the animals. They were more interested in the camels. The landlord had owned elephants before, but these were the first camels that had ever set foot in the village. The villagers thought that they looked funny. The skinny legs, the humped backs, the thin long necks and especially the sleepy looking oval head perched on the long necks. The sleepy faces gave the camels a lazy look, and the jaws seemed to be perennially chewing.

“Look at the necks”, someone commented, “they look ugly”.

"The skinny legs look as if there is only bone and no flesh on them".

"I wonder What's in the hump?"

"It stores water".

"If it stored water in the hump, it wouldn't be as hard as a rock".

"How do you know that it's hard as a rock?"

"It looks as hard as a rock".

"It is called the ship of the desert", commented a short person.

"It doesn't look anything like a ship, then why call it the ship of the desert?".

"Don't know, ask an educated person".

"Shush, Gopesh babu is coming."

Everyone fell silent as an important person walked through the crowd who made way for him. He walked past the rows of spectators and stopped at the first rung.

"Pranaam Gopesh Babu", the crowd greeted the newcomer in unison.

"Namastay", the important person wished back as he stood with his legs astride with one hand holding an end of the dhoti (holding an end of the dhoti was a sign of importance). He was of medium height and wore an expensive thin fabricated dhoti from under which his bottom seemed to peep. His torso was hidden under a silk kurta and he had short cropped hair with a three inch long pigtail called a "teek" hanging from the back of his head. To enhance his important look, he seemed to have cultivated a huge paunch which protruded from under his kurta.

He was the village doctor, or precisely the learned quack. His clinic was situated in the heart of the village and boasted of medical certificates aquired from prestigious colleges from all over India when actually the important gentleman had seen education only till class ten. Infact he had failed in his matriculation examinations. Anyway for the villagers he was the learned doctor, since they did not know what a quack was. The gentleman had worked for sometime as a compounder in the city for a doctor who had a roaring medical practice and had returned to the village enlightened.

"How do you like the animals doctor sahib?", a humble bare backed villager asked.

"Impressive", replied the learned quack who was really impressed. He looked at the villagers, at the people whose near and dear ones he had sent out of their earthly existence much before the life span allotted to them by the almighty had ended. His twangy lotions which was a mixture of allopathy and Ayurveda recipes soaked in cows piss ·generally misfired and bushfired and sent the recipients flying out of their earthly bodies into an irritated almighties lap who just did not know what to do with the quack. He kept throwing up the villagers souls just when the almighty did not want them.

"How are you Rajesh babu, how is your asthma?", questioned the doctor to an elderly gentleman.

"It's become worse doctor, I find it more difficult to breathe". Rajesh babu was a villager who was suffering form Asthma. The quacks lotion of cows piss mixed with donkeys hair with a pinch of cow dung to purify it, seemed to have aggravated the Asthma.

"Don't worry", the quack consoled the asthmic gentleman. "The medicine is working perfectly. It will first aggravate the disease, intensify it, then completely wipe it out, so have patience."

A month later the patient Rajesh Babu was completely wiped out.

"We are very lucky and should be grateful to our respected zemindar for bringing to our village these two animals", the learned quack commented.

The villagers and Jehangir looked perplexed. They did not understand why the two camels were so important. What could the camels do except to pull a cart or two or be show pieces?

"Camels piss', continued the quack as his paunch grew bigger due to the attention he was attracting. "Camels piss is a potent medicine and can cure many illnesses. It makes a person resistant to the different strains of fever especially malaria. If you rub the liquid on your skin, it will make the latter as soft as a new born babies. If you drink it, it will cure coughs colds, bronchitis, arthritis, whooping coughs, stomach disorders, falaria, malaria and many other diseases including cancer".

This was too much for the villagers. They looked at the learned quack, then suddenly turned and scampered off leaving the learned gentleman standing alone with Jehangir.

"Doctor sahib we are very lucky", commented Jehangir.

"Yes, very, very lucky".

The crowd was back with each person holding a bottle.

The quack held out a hand to a short bare bodied boy. "Can I have your bottle?", he asked. "You can go back to your home and fetch another one".

Anything was done to oblige the respected doctor so the boy handed over the bottle and scampered off to fetch another one. In the meantime the crowd and the learned doctor waited for the camels to piddle and chatted as they did so. They discussed politics and the departure of the quacks latest victim. The latter had been a learned person and was one of the elders of the village, and had been full of old stories which he narrated till the day he died. The quacks lotion of Allopathic what not, mixed with Ayurvedic what not, dipped in cows piss, and purified in cow dung had sent the soul shooting out of his earthly existence, through the land of the dead to finally sit on the almighties lap from where it looked down in disgust at the quack who was hammering away at the dead persons chest, desperately trying to bring the heart back to life. He blamed the tragic departure on the heart and not his own twangy lotions. To make matters worse, an equally irritated almighty was totally disinterested in the stories the recent arrival tried to narrate about the oldies of the village, and wanted to throw the irritating soul right back to earth and the quack.

The male camel looked around and gave a loud "Brrrump".

That was the signal and the learned doctor rushed forward to what was now an open tap. He put the bottle in line with the flowing liquid, collected a bottle full and moved back as he re-corked the bottle. This was the signal for the rest to collect their share, and knowing that the bladder had a limited amount which was not enough for everyone, the crowd rushed in and shoved and pushed and pulled to somehow collect some of the potent liquid which spilled onto hands, vests, kurta's, dhoti's, anywhere but the bottles.

The surprised male camel craned its long neck around to see what was happening below its piddling self. The female camel turned around, belched, and wondered what the humans were upto as they squabbled under the male camels underbelly. The cows understood what was happening since they were used to the humans stealing from their piddling selves. The baby elephant cocked its head sideways, and flapped its huge ears wondering what the humans were upto. He did not realize that the quack had proved that the camels were a walking, belching, hay eating, cheap pharmaceutical plant.

The humans were behaving like a bottling plant.
The camels piss had just been proved divine.
The humans shouted "It is mine, it is mine".

Life In The Cowshed

The next day Jehangir got up late and sliding out his warm haystack hole, he brushed his hair and twirled his huge whiskers making them flow towards his ears. Taking his lota, he filled it with water and taking the gun he went to the field to defecate. After doing the needful, he washed his hands and scrubbed his teeth with a mango stick as he walked upto the camels. The baby elephant was standing alone in the "Haathikhana", swishing its trunk, flapping its ears and blowing mud over its back.

"Malla Prasad", Jehangir grinned. "It's a nice name." He walked to the Haathikhana and laid the double barrel shotgun on the ground.

There was a crowd standing in a circle around the two camels and every person had a bottle in his hand and was waiting patiently for the animals to urinate. The sleepy looking camels had in fact become the star attractions and the cows had also started commenting on how handsome they looked, and how macho their long legs and skinny necks were.

"Look how they stand high", drooled a light gray cow who was pregnant. "They look so handsome, so smart".

"Look at their legs, they look strong and sturdy", commented a short Frezian cow who had fallen in love.

Now this was not liked by the bull, who didn't like the idea of his wives passing adoring remarks at other males, so he shook his horns and charged. The humans scampered to a safe distance while the jealous creature snorted and showed the camels its horns.

"Why is he behaving like that?", asked the camel, "the cows have adjusted themselves to our presence?, then why is he behaving in that way?"

"He's scared that you will run away with one of them, that's why he's showing you his horns. He's jealous of you and your looks", commented the stallion. "That's why they call him a male chauvinist pig."

"But its sheer foolishness", replied the male camel, "you can see we aren't made for each other. Those cows would hardly reach my belly. Look at my long legs and neck, and look at theirs.

"I don't care if you are made for each other or not", snorted the bull. "All I care is you stay away from my wives in future".

"But I never went any where near them".

"Don't speak back to me", ordered the bull as it rushed forward, "or I'll smash your skinny legs out of shape".

The camel was now nervous and moved back belching to Jehangir to do something.

"Now you gal's in there", the bull had turned to the cowshed and was belching at the cows. "If I see any of you winking or passing lurid comments, or showering flying kisses at those long legged insects, I'll blacken your faces, ram into your heads, chew off your ears and make you look so ugly that one would care to give you a second glance, so take care and beware".

Jehangir arrived with a huge stick and thwacked the bull on its rump, sending the irritated bovine belching and lumbering off. Throwing the stick he walked upto the group of bottle holding men and asked them to name the animals. "I asked the mistress to do so," he said, "but she refused, she finds the camels ugly".

"She may find the camels ugly", said a man holding a bottle. "She has a lot of money to buy medicines. For us poor people, the camels look beautiful, especially because of the potent medicine they have".

"How about giving them a name", advised Jehangir, "the baby elephant already has one. His name is Malla Prasad".

A tall lanky villager in a vest and dhoti spoke up. "Since these camels provide us such cheap medicines", he suggested, "lets give them a medical name, like the names of those big pharmaceutical companies".

"I got one', commented a person who was wearing a pair of old bell bottoms which ill fitted him. "Let's call the female camel Glaxo".

"Good, good", commented another, "and the male one?".

"Ranbaxy, how was that?".

"Doesn't sound as good as Glaxo."

"Okay then Hoechst"

"It sounds funny; it twists the tongue".

"Brufen is a tablet which shooes away body aches. How is that for a name?"

"Yes Brufen will do," interceded Jehangir. "The male camel from now on is Brufen, the female is Glaxo and the elephant is Malla Prasad".

"I can hear a jeep coming," commented a little boy who was standing in his birth day clothes. Everyone fell silent as the drone of a jeeps engine grew louder.

"It is the master returning ," shouted Jehangir as

he ran towards the Haathikhana to fetch his shot gun. "Jogi go and open the gates", he ordered.

Jogi ran off towards the twin lioned gate while Jehangir slung the gun over his shoulder and walked towards the verandah while the villagers except fora few ran off. Those who remained were adamant to capture some of the potent liquid and had decided to ask the zemindar's permission to do so.

"Well then we have a name", commented the male camel. "I am Brufen, you are Glaxo, and the little one there is Malla Prasad." Then turning to the horses he asked, "Do the two of you also have names?"

"Yes", said the stallion, "I am Raja and she is Rani".

"The bulls?"

"I don't know what the humans call them, but the cows have given them names".

"What are they?".

"They are Headache, Bodyache, Legache, Muscleache, Rumpache, Neckache, Hornache, and Hoofache".

"Haw, haw, haw", belched Brufen and Glaxo together.

"Haw, haw, haw", hawed the cows.

"And the cows", asked Glaxo, "what are they called?"

"They have an assortment of names", answered the mare. "That is Buttercup there, and the short one is Cherry blossom, and she is next to Cauliflower. She's the one with the long horns and."

"Look the master is coming", interrupted a cow.

Jehangir Khan and the manager were walking a step behind Avadesh Prasad, "Nice names", commented the master, "the villagers are very imaginative. How is the baby elephant?"

Very naughty master.

"Jehangir, there is enough fodder for the cows and the camels. I want you to take special care of the elephant", then turning around to his manager, Avadesh asked "Munsiji, is there a plot of land lying fallow?".

The little bespectacled manager was always carrying a note pad and pen. He was short, wore a dhoti and kurta and had rubber slippers under his feet. His name was Munsi Mahavir Lal and he belonged to the Kayastha community, a caste of pen pusher's owing allegiance to lord Chitragupta, the god of the Munsif's. "There is sir", he answered.

"Where?"

"On the banks of the Ganges."

"Lets see it."

The three walked to the waiting jeep and climbed in Avadesh sat in front while the manager and Jehangir piled into the back.

"Have you got your gun Jehangir?", Avadesh asked.

"Yes sir."

"Good."

The driver started the engine and pulled out of the double lioned gate. After traveling a little distance the jeep reached an intersection where it turned right and traveled along a rutted dirt track along which the driver cautiously kept the wheels out of the ruts. The jeep sped on along the paddy fields till it reached the banks of the river with the water flowing twenty feet below.

The vehicle stopped and the zemindar got out just as a few bare bodied dark people came running over.

They were ryots and they bent down low and namastayed the zemindar. Jehangir and the manager climbed down after the master, and the little group found themselves standing in a fifteen acre plot of land which was lying fallow.

"This is the plot sir."

"The zemindar walked to the river bank and looked across the water's to the gentle sand dunes flowing alongside the river on the other side where he owned three hundred acres of land. The river looked majestic as it gurgled past the landlord. It seemed to be whispering a namastay.

"Jehangir," Avadesh called.

"Yes master."

"I hear the naxalites have reached these areas also."

"I have also heard master."

"Problem clouds are hovering over us, it seems."

"Yes master."

The group watched a steamer pass. It belonged to the Indian railways, and was of 1910 vintage. It ferried passenger's from Bhagalpur to Patna, and its huge paddle wheels lazily splatted the water, pushing the huge boat forward.

"What should I do?"

"Fight for what you think is right master."

The zemindar turned around and pointed to the fallow land. "I am handing over this plot to you. Get the tractor and get it ploughed and grow sugar cane in it. It will be solely for the elephant's consumption. It must'nt be sold in the market. Do you understand?"

"Yes sir."

"Can I trust you?"

"I will try to be honest sir."

"Good." The zemindar climbed back into the jeep. The driver climbed in and switched on the ignition. The engine coughed to life just as Jehangir and the manager piled in. The driver shifted the gear to forward and the jeep was soon moving along the rutted road it had just come along, after the rear wheels had thrown mud and grit on the ryots who had been left behind. Turning his head around Avadesh ordered the manager, "Munsiji, pay Jehangir the money necessary to cultivate the field."

"Yes sir."

The jeep drove back into the double lioned gate and stopped in front of the verandah. The zemindar got out and ordered the driver to help Jehangir in whatever way it was possible. "When he needs the tractor, you don't have to ask for my permission, just plough the field for him."

With the gun still hanging from his shoulder, Jehangir twirled his mustache and walked past the cowshed to the Haathikhana. Caressing the head of the elephant, he told the latter the good news. "Do you know Malla Prasad", he said, "Do you know that you are now the zemindar of fifteen acres of land." The little pachyderm shook its head as if to say "no."

"You are the zemindar of fifteen acres of sugar care. You are much richer than me and Jogi."

The bare backed Jogi walked upto Jehangir. "Have you finished milking the cow's?", asked Jehangir, "If so, then get ready to come with me to the riverside. The master has allotted fifteen acres of land to grow sugar. This is for the elephants consumption."

Jehangir washed the elephant and taking the driver and tractor, he supervised the ploughing of the field.

Sugar cane was sown and in a couple of months a huge Jungle had come up on the allotted plot. It was Jehangir's job to take the little elephant daily to the cane field, hack some cane and load it on its back, and bring it back to the Haathikhana where he would strip the cane off its leaves which where put in front of the camels to eat. The elephant enjoyed the sweet cane and looked forward to the little walk to the riverside and back.

Of course the bulls were jealous and the news gave them more reason to show their horns. The poor pachyderm was terrified when ever it was confronted by them. "Why do they behave in such a manner", asked the elephant. "They don't seem to get along with anyone in this compound."

"They are bulls", replied the stallion. "They are made head strong, so don't pay attention to them."

The years passed as summers followed spring, and monsoon followed summer. Malla Prasad was the chief guest amongst the animals. He was given special treatment by Jehangir and the master and he loved the yellow ball's called laddooe's when ever the fat mistress came to pray to him. He daily looked forward to her arrival with the skinny Shiela in tow.

Time passed and Jehangir Khan lost more hair from his head, the mistress grew fatter, Jogi grew into a strong young man and a thief who pilfered milk from the udder's of the master's cows, Headache died and was carted away to be replaced by a younger more tempestuous Headache, the camel couple gave birth to a baby male camel whom the villager's named Ranbaxy, Brufen was one day found lying dead, Ranbaxy grew up into a strong male camel, Bodyache and Rumpache were carted away to be eaten by mangy dogs and vulture's and were replaced by younger and more virile Bodyache's and Rumpache's. Malla Prasad daily went with Jehangir Khan to the cane field and brought back cane, Glaxo gave birth to a skinny female camel which the villagers named Cadilla, the camels complained that they never peed on the ground but always in bottles, news of naxalite atrocities filtered in, and Malla Prasad grew into a beautiful, strong young male elephant with a long trunk, broad round legs, and huge ears. He was around nine feet tall, and had grown a pair of beautiful milky white tusks.

The bulls were now scared of the elephant and stayed away from him. They showed him their horn's from a safe distance and that also only when he was tied to stakes dug in the ground. Younger bulls took the place of the older ones and the horse couple though much older now, remained childless. "So Malla", they neighed, "how do you feel?"

"Fine", replied the elephant, "its only that I feel lonely."

"Why?"

"Every animal here is a couple. There are males and females for every one. I feel lonely and desire a female."

"Ho, ho, ho, jumbo wants a mate," belched Headache," any one for marriage? Jumbo wants a mate."

"Yes I want a mate, so shut up."

"Okay, okay, don't get angry, " then turning aside the bull cackled." Heh, heh, heh, Jumbo wants a mate, anyone for marriage?"

"I warn you bulls, I might one day kick one of you

to death."

"Your predecessor did that once ", neighed the mare.

"My predecessor did that once?, what do you mean?"

"You weren't told this because we were told that elephants are scared of ghosts."

"Yes I am scared of ghosts."

"Well there was an elephant who lived where you live now. He died a year before you were brought here. He was a male like you, and felt lonely just like you. I don't understand why the human's did not give him a mate. Anyway he did not like the bulls and the bulls did not like him. One day one of the bulls, a particularly nasty one charged at him from the back and rammed into his left hind leg."

The mare stopped for a second.

"Then what happened?"

"Not much. The elephant lifted its right hind leg and rammed the sole against the bull's head. The fellow didn't even belch or kick in death throes. He simply slumped down dead".

"What happened to my predecessor?"

"Don't know, one morning he never got up and Jehangir tried to wake him up. He was lying dead on the same spot where you are standing now."

"What did they do to the dead body?", asked Malla Prasad, "was it fed to the dogs and vultures?"

"No," replied the mare. "Do you see that little hill against the boundary wall?"

"Yes,"

"That is the grave of the elephant called Paddum Prasad."

Laal Salaam

The month of April in Bihar is extremely hot. It is a season which the Bihari's love, when the heavy woolen's are discarded and the stuffed gunny sacks are thrown away and the people again move around in thin fabriqued bottom peeping dhoti's, a vest and a thin kurta. The hot westerly wind called the loo blows its hot breath over the land, ripening mangoes, drying up lakes and pond's and making the paddy fields take a yellowish golden hue as it passes. The loo was a happier loo during the Raj days when the first signs of its hot breath would send the English master's packing to the hill resorts of Darjeeling, Simla and Mussorie. These Bihari's were different, they were stubborn. They in fact waited for it and rejoiced when it came, because it brought the harvesting season with it. This is a season of plenty when rural Bihar becomes extremely busy. No one has time for guests or to travel. Everyone is busy harvesting the Ravi crop. This was a busy season too for the extremist communists groups who called themselves naxalites. The country side was covered in yellow gold and snatching land from the landed was most profitable now. They not only took the land. As a bonus, they took the harvest also.

"Ladies, friends, and gentleman", boomed a loud voice, "for how many years are you going to toil as slaves?. For how long, will you work for the profits of the landed aristocrats".

The person bellowing was a tall broad shouldered

dark man called Bhalua. He was bare backed and was wearing a half dhoti which did not go beyond his thighs and his chocolaty brown skin glistened with the April morning perspiration. He was speaking in the square of a little hamlet called Bijulia which was on the other side of the Ganges from Ramnagar. The village did not have any pucca houses, only thatched ones and the dusty village square was where the villagers met, where there was a makeshift wooden dais for the speaker. The village was surrounded by paddy fields which belonged to the residents of upper caste Ramnagar and half of the land belonged to zemindar Avadesh Prasad Singh. The residents of Bijulia were of the Harijan community and relied on the Bhumihar Brahmin landlords of Ramnagar for their livelihood.

"What is land?", bellowed Bhalua. "Land is a part of the earth which is our heritage and was gifted to mankind by the almighty. This earth belongs to everyone, rich and poor alike. How come people corner large plots of land and say this is mine and this is yours. I repeat. Land belongs to every living being on this earth and not to a few chosen humans only".

The crowd that had gathered to listen started murmuring. They liked the sounds emanating from naxalite Bhalua's mouth.

"The Government", Bhalua shouted. "Is a government made by the landed aristocrats to further their own needs. It is a government manned by rich bureaucrats who are fed by the landed aristocrats. The government is a dictatorship in the garb of a democracy. It is a farce".

The crowd murmured in approval.

"It has been thirty years since this country gained

independence. The constitution was framed, and what did they call it? `For the people, by the people and off the people'. I want to ask each of you - What did you get from this, `for the people government?' Do you own the land that you live in?, Do you own the fields that you plough?, Do you own the cow tied in front of your huts?, Do you have electricity?, Do you have water?, Do you have medical facilities to save your children from diseases? There is a big "NO" to all these questions. You do not own anything other than the miserable souls inside your miserable bodies".

"Yes", murmured the crowd. "The person speaks for us".

"Then what do we do?", an onlooker shouted.

"FIGHT", bellowed Bhalua. Fight for your rights. You have to take what is yours with your own hands. Don't wait for the government to give you pittances and doles. This government was made for the landed aristocrats. They give you pittances to keep you in good humor and to stay in power themselves. Tell them that you don't want the pittances and the miserable government doles. Tell them that you want land. Land to call your own, land that your children can call their own, land that will give you a house to live in, land that will clothe you and land that will provide medical treatment to you and your young ones".

"Yes", shouted a villager who was wearing a yellow turban and was bare bodied. "WE want land", then turning to his fellow villager's he bellowed. "We want the land that we toil in. The fields around our village belong to us. LONG LIVE THE RED REVOLUTION", he hollered.

"Long live the red revolution", the villagers hollered

back.

"A thin stubby naxalite with only one eye got up and silenced the crowd. "Silence comrades", he screamed. "First listen to what comrade Bhalua has to say".

"The revolution", hollered Bhalua. "The red revolution has spread over the state of West Bengal. It started from a little village called Naxalbari and spread to the whole of the state. The landless are now owners of the soil and the landlords are either dead or have fled to Calcutta. We are now attempting to spread the revolution in Bihar and have been successful to a certain extent. Most of the landlords and zemindar's are in hiding or have fled, except for a few like the pig Avadesh Prasad Singh. It is our job to bring these landlord's to heel and take what is rightfully ours".

"Comrade Bhalua zindabad", a villager shouted.

"Comrade Bhalua zindabad", the villagers shouted back.

The one eyed jack once more got up and screamed at the crowd to be silent. "Let comrade Bhalua finish his speech", he yelled.

The crowd fell silent.

"Now tell me", Bhalua hollered. "Are you ready to fight?".

"Yes", screamed back the onlookers.

"Are you ready to kill for what is yours?".

"Yes".

"There are no cowards amongst us?".

"No".

"Comrade Ganesh, please bring out the prisoners".

The one eyed jack got up and walked to a hut in front of which Bhalua was standing and opened the thatched door. "Come out", he ordered.

Three people with their hands tied behind their backs were led out. One was thin and short and wore rubber slippers and was bespectacled. He was munsif Mahavir Lal, the manager of zemindar Avadesh Prasad Singh's estate. The other two were heavily built and were the zemindar's pehelwans and were incharge of the land near the village. The three were pushed to stand in front of comrade Bhalua.

"Do you recognize these gentelemen?", bellowed Bhalua.

"Yes", screamed the onlookers.

"These three are the representatives of the zemindar? Am I right?".

"Yes".

"Today they are standing in front of you. Your court, the people's court".

"What is a people's court?", yelled back a bare bodied villager.

"A people's court is a place where instant justice is imparted. It is not like the government courts where they take years to decide on what do do. The trial is short, and the people pass the verdict".

The one eyed jack got up and yelled. "These three people are the representatives of the zemindar and have been suppressing you all these years. They suppressed in the name of the zemindar, and in the process, they filled their own pockets also. Am I right?"

"Yes, screamed a bald onlooker. "kill them, kill them".

"Wait, wait, wait", yelled the one eyed Jack. "We will deal with them one by one". Pointing to the tallest person, he ordered a comrade to untie him. "Now tell me comrades. Is this tall man guilty?", he asked.

"Yes", screamed back the crowd.

"What did he do?".

"He plundered and looted us. He did not hesitate to bully us in the name of the zemindar".

"What should his punishment be?".

"Death", the crowd roared back.

"Wait a minute, wait a minute", yelled an elderly gray haired, bare bodied villager. "Let me also speak".

"Yes let him speak", shouted some people.

The old gentleman walked upto the makeshift dais on which comrade Bhalua stood and climbed on. He raised a clenched fist at Bhalua as a salam which Bhalua returned by raising his own clenched fist. "Friends and noble villagers", he shouted, "lets not be rash and hot headed. We must not forget that we are humans and that there is something called humanity. I know these gentlemen have been inhuman to us, but that doesn't mean that we should draw blood. I am not against comrade Bhalua or his group and his methods. It is just that I don't like killing. That does not mean that we will not fight for our rights. Whether these men live or die, we will take over the lands that surround our village. But let us not be the first ones to kill. Let us give the zemindar a chance. We will take his lands and if he comes to fight then only will we fight back. We will fight with all our might, and cursed is the man who will run away".

Bhalua shook his head. "This gentleman here thinks that zemindar Avadesh Prasad Singh is lily livered", he shouted, "He thinks he is a pansy. He does not realize that most of the landlords of Bihar have escaped to Patna. They now reside there and live far away from their lands. Avadesh Prasad is one of the few who have preferred to stay away from the safety of the cities. He lives here and is prepared to face the danger that we will pose to him".

"I accept what ever comrade Bhalua says", interrupted the old man. "I know he has been fighting the landlords and he knows their ways more than me, but I still vote to spare these three peoples lives. It isn't necessary to kill them. We must concentrate on our main goal. That is land. Let these three people go. They will tell the zemindar how angry we are".

"I don't accept it", shouted Bhalua, "I don't accept what this old comrade has to say. After what these three people did to you, do you still think they should go away completely free?".

"I am not suggesting to let them go completely free", shouted the elderly gentleman. "They should receive some sort of punishment for what they did to us. But it isn't necessary to kill them. Kill only when it is necessary".

Turning to the old man Bhalua asked. "What punishment should we give them?"

"Let them run a gauntlet", replied the old man. "Every able bodied man or boy will take a fat stick and stand in two rows. These three gentlemen will run through them one at a time and they will be beaten with the sticks. If they run through the gauntlet, they will be free to cross the river and go back to the zemindar's mansion. However if they fall or faint, their bodies will be thrown on the other side of the river".

"Yes", roared back the crowd and scampered off to fetch sticks. They assembled in two long lines. Bhalua got down form the dais and opened the first persons rope and freed his hands. The person was elderly and heavily built and wore a dhoti and kurta, but was barefoot.

"Okay now run".

The person dashed into the two rows of villagers and ran as people took swings at him, some hitting him, while others missed.

"Don't hit his head", shouted the old man, "Hit anywhere except for the head".

The man went on running as people swung their sticks at him. One stick hit his shin causing him to stumble and fall. The people closest to him rained blows on his back and bottom as he got up and continued running. He was soon safely out of the gauntlet.

"Continue running", shouted the old man, "or we may catch you and drag you back. And tell the zemindar that these lands are no longer his, they our ours".

The pehelwan dashed off and disappeared into the lanes and by lanes of the village.

Bhalua walked over to the second person who was tall, dark and thin. He looked athletic and wore sandals and a dhoti and kurta. Opening the rope that tied his hands, he ordered him to run. The person dashed off and was soon being hit by sticks.

"Break his bones", yelled Bhalua.

"Break his legs", yelled another person.

The thin gentleman went on running, trying to dodge the sticks. Soon he was out of the gauntlet and was running through the lanes and by by-lines of the village, desperate to get out of the area and cross the Ganges to safety.

Bhalua walked over to the cowering bespectacled Mahavir lal and opening his rope, he ordered him to run.

"No my son please no", cried the manager. "Have mercy on me. I'm not built like the other two".

Bhalua pushed the terrified person. "Run you pig", he ordered.

The munsif fell at Bhalua's feet. "Son have mercy on me, I won't be able to bear those sticks".

Catching the munsif by the hair and picking him up Bhalua slapped the latter causing his spectacles to fly off and fall on the ground. Then pushing the munsif forward he ordered him to run. "Run or I'll kick you", shouted Bhalua.

"Stop it", ordered the old man who had just spared the three peoples lives. Bending down he picked up the spectacles and put them on the manager's face. "Let him go", he ordered. "He is too small and too frail to withstand the gauntlet".

"Comrade, you are too forgiving".

"What will you get by beating or hitting him. Look at the frightened look on his face. He is already dead. Let the man go".

The gauntletiers put down their sticks and made way for the terrified manager who was shaking like an electronic vibrator. The terrified munsif did not unfold his folded hands as he slowly and suspiciously walked off.

"I apologize to comrade Bhalua if he thinks that I tried to supersede him", apologized the old man.

Bhalua went back to stand on the dais. "The three prisoners have been dealt with", he yelled, "now to continue our business. The two pehelwans resided in this village. Lets burn the house in which they lived".

"Why burn the house", shouted back the old man. "Why not make it our head office, or a branch office of the peoples war group".

"Excellent", shouted Bhaḷua. Then pointing a finger at the one eyed Ganesh and two others who were wearing only half dhoti's, he continued. "My comrade here will teach you how to fight. We do not have guns so they will teach you how to make bows and arrows and how to use them. They will also teach you how to fight with axes and spears. Do you understand?"

"Yes", shouted the crowd.

"Then lift your hands up and clench your fists and shout with me, LONG LIVE THE RED REVOLUTION".

"LONG LIVE THE RED REVOLUTION", the crowed shouted back.

"That will not do", shouted Bhalua, "shout out louder so that the sound waves will reverberate through the wheat fields and through the mango groves to the other side of the river bringing fear into the hearts of the people living in the mansions.

"LONG LIVE THE RED REVOLUTION", he hollered.

"LONG LIVE THE RED REVOLUTION", the crowd hollered back.

"Good", bellowed Bhalua. "LAAL SALAAM", he screamed.

"LAAL SALAAM", screamed back the crowd.

The old gray haired man climbed back onto the dais. "Now every one of you take your sickles and lets go into our fields and harvest our wheat", he suggested.

Bhalua smiled. "Yes comrades, the old man is right.

Take your sickles every man and woman and lets harvest our fields. Every man will own every grain of wheat he harvests".

THE ZEMINDAR HITS BACK

Tied in the haathikhana Malla Prasad waited patiently for the mahout to come. He was looking forward to the little walk to the cane field he owned on the banks of the Ganges. Seeing the bald Jehangir come around the verandah corner, the elephant lifted its trunk and trumpeted.

"I'm coming I'm coming", shouted Jehangir.

"It's your lucky day today Malla", belched Glaxo, "I will be waiting for my share of the tall grass".

"I wish he would take you along too", mumbled Malla Prasad.

As usual Jehangir had his gun slung over his right shoulder from a strap and the cartridge studded belt across his chest. "Come on Malla", he said as he bent down to open the iron shackles which kept the elephant tied to the wooden stakes. He was at ease walking amongst the huge feet as he unshackled each of them. Malla Prasad had grown to his full height so Jehangir no longer led him around by holding his ears. He had a little three foot long iron spear with him which was pointed on both ends and had a hook on one side. The mahouts called this a Gajra and used it to poke the elephants head or the root of the huge ears to make the latter obey their orders.

Malla Prasad now understood the human language and the few elephantish words which were used to talk to him. He knew that when Jehangir pulled his tail or his trunk and said "Agath" it meant to move forward. If he did the same uttering the words "Pichoo hut", it meant to move back. "Chaiy, meant sit down and "maiy", meant to stand up. "Utha", meant that he should pick up something with his trunk.

After the legs were unshackled, Jehangir put down his gun and taking a pair of brass bells which were tied to both ends of a five foot long rope, he climbed up the trunk, and perching himself on the head, he let the bells hang from the elephants neck. He then shinnied down the trunk and walked into the Haathikhana and picked up an axe and a sharp dhow. Picking up a bundle of rope he ordered the elephant to sit down. "Malla Prasad chaiy", he ordered. "Chaiy, Malla, chaiy."

Malla Prasad obeyed and let down his bottom as his hind legs bent. His head was still high up, so he bent his fore legs and made them lie on the ground, thereby lowering himself. Jehangir swung the rope onto the bare back and hung the spiked Gajra from a ear and taking the gun, he climbed onto the head and sat astride the neck. "Malla Prasad 'Maiy' ", he ordered as he nudged the base of the ears with his toe. "Maiy Malla Maiy."

The elephant gave a soft rumble and lifted the right ankle. The left ankle followed suite and as the bells tinkled, the pachyderm heaved up bringing the fore legs in a standing position. The head had moved up but the bottom was still sloped down so heaving his hind legs up, he lifted his bottom and straightened himself as the bells again tinkled. Malla Prasad was on all his fours. The stomach gently swayed to the left as the bells tinkled again and the elephant walked out of the Haathikhana, past the camel, past the cowshed and the adoring horned heads, past the irritated bulls and into the courtyard which faced the white mansion. Turning right towards the double lioned gate he walked on past the double lion's that had frightened him long ago.

"Didn't he look majestic", mooed a cow.

"Marvelous", mooed another.

"Robust", belched another.

"Insect", belched the bull, "he looked like an overgrown insect, and stop drooling over him. You are my harem, so behave like a harem. You aren't supposed to look at any other male other than me."

"The bulls behave so foolishly", belched Glaxo, "they talk just like MALE CHAUVINIST PIGS."

Malla Prasad had reached the crossroad and had turned right taking the path that led to the Ganges. Seeing him, scared dogs whined and scampered off with their tails between their legs. Cows in nearby fields belched and ran off. Bullocks panicked and ran with their carts trundling behind them. People working in fields stopped work to watch the graceful, lordly animal pass. Sitting on the neck and bobbing with the soft bobbing motion of the head, Jehangir gently "Agathed", his ward on as he gently nudged the base of the ears with his feet. Malla Prasad flapped his ears as he obeyed and perched proudly on the neck, Jehangir felt like a King sitting astride a Majestic animal. No one dared block his route. Everyone or everything moved off the road to let the majestic couple pass.

Reaching the sugar cane field, Jehangir threw the rope, axe and dhow to the ground as he himself climbed down the trunk. "You wait here", he ordered "while I cut the sugar cane."

Taking the dhow he walked into the cane field and started hacking at the stems. As he worked Malla Prasad took a handful of dust into his trunk and lifting it above his head he sprayed it over his back. "That should disturb the fleas," he rumbled then taking some more mud he swished the trunk in a circle spraying the air with the dust.

Hacking at the sugar cane stem, Jehangir looked up and realized that Malla Prasad had dirtied himself. Adjusting his gun which had slid down, he dropped the dhow and walked over to the elephant. "There you have dove it again", he scolded, "you sometimes behave like a street urchin." Taking hold of the trunk he turned the elephant around and led him to the edge of the river. Walking down the sandy incline he led the animal into the water. "Now I will have to give you a bath", he said, "or the master will become angry if he see's you in this state."

Knee deep in the water Malla Prasad let his hind legs buckle allowing his rear to come down. The fore legs were allowed to fold and the elephant was soon sitting in the water, and taking the liquid in its trunk it squirted it on Jehangir's bald pate.

"Now why did you have to do that for?", complained the mahout as he pulled up his lungi till it was only till his knee. Putting down his gun he waded into the water and proceeded to scrub the coarse grayish black skin with a piece of wet cloth. "You love this bath don't you Malla", the mahout commented as he rubbed.

Malla Prasad knew what Jehangir wanted so he lay on his side as the latter scrubbed his huge underbelly.

After scrubbing for some time the mahout felt tired so he waded out of the water to where his gun and belt were. Sitting down on his haunches he pulled out a tobacco pouch from his breast pocket and taking the tobacco out, he mixed it with lime and proceeded to rub it in his hands when something on the other side of the river attracted his attention. There were three men on the opposite bank desperately waving at him. The wind was blowing in their direction so Jehangir could not hear what they were shouting. He picked up the belt and strapped it across his chest and tightened the buckles. Picking up the gun, he hurried into the water and shouted at the elephant to get up.

A surprised Malla Prasad who was lolling in the water looked up at him. The eyes seemed to ask, "what is it?"

"Maiy, malla maiy", shouted Jehangir. The way the three people were frantically waving told the mahout that something was badly wrong.

Malla Frasad straightened into a sitting position and catching the huge left ear Jehangir climbed onto the head and sat down with his legs straddling the neck. "Maiy Malla Maiy", he shouted as he unhooked the spiked spear from the right ear and poked the elephant on the head.

The legs heaved up sending the head and front shoulder blades up. Soon the bottom followed suite and prodding with his toes behind the ear, Jehangir shouted "Agath."

The elephant stood still for a moment not comprehending the order. "Agath", meant move forward, but the river was in front and the deep water's were just thirty feet away.

"Agath agath", shouted Jehangir as he kicked the ear base and spiked the head softly. "Agath."

"But the river is in front of us", mumbled the elephant, "How do I go forward?"

Jehangir understood the elephants hesitation and climbed down the trunk. Taking hold of it and shouting "Agath", he led the elephant into the water. Malla Prasad now understood that the mahout wanted him to cross the river so he willingly moved forward as Jehangir climbed back onto the neck. "We have done this before Malla", he said. "Come on agath agath".

The elephant waded into the river till it was chest deep in. It carried on as the soft river bed dipped, bringing the elephant lower into the water till only the head and back were discernible. The pachyderm lifted its trunk and went deeper into the water till it was totally submerged, with only the trunk protruding out while Jehangir stood balancing himself on the submerged back. For sometime it looked like Jehangir and the trunk were sailing through the water, with the pachyderm breathing strongly through the trunk. However the river bed soon curved upwards and more of the trunk emerged from the water. Soon the tip of the curved back came out and Jehangir could seat himself again. Slowly as the water shallowed more of the elephant emerged and Malla Prasad was soon walking in ankle deep water.

The two heavier built men ran up while the thin short manager lagged behind.

"What is it?", shouted Jehangir.

"Bring the elephant down quick", ordered the pehelwans. "This side of the river has become dangerous. It has become naxalite territory."

"Chaiy Malla Chaiy", Jehangir ordered as the elephant proceeded to sit down on its belly.

The pehelwans climbed on as Munsif Mahavir Lal huffed and puffed upto the elephant. "Lets get out of here fast", he ordered as Jehangir pulled him up.

Jehangir shouted "Maiy", and the elephant heaved itself up. He pulled the left ear and the elephant turned around and walked back to the river and into the deep waters taking the four people safely to the opposite bank.

"Quick", ordered Mahavir Lal, "go back straight to the mansion. A communist rebellion has just taken place on the other side. The ryots have taken over the masters and the village's lands."

Jehangir kicked into the base of the ears and the elephant rushed up the incline to the hard ground.

"Forget the road", ordered Mahavir Lal, "travel in a straight line towards the mansion. Travel across the fields as the crow flies."

Jehangir directed Malla Prasad across the fields and trampled through then not taking notice of the irritated farmers who shouted at him. It was an emergency. It was the crunch. The fight he and his master had dreaded for so long had come.

It was a surprised zemindar who saw the elephant barge in through his open gates and stop in front of the verandah where he was sitting. Before the Pachyderm could sit down the two pehelwans had jumped off and were namastaying him. "Master", they shouted, "the ryots of Bijulia have rebelled. They say that those lands are no more yours. It now belongs to them. They captured us and tried us in their weird court. We were sentenced to death, but were saved by an old ryot called Ram Singh who said that it wasn't necessary to kill us. All they wanted was to take possession of your wheat fields."

Avadesh Prasad went pale. He glanced at Jehangir, then at the other's "Have they taken over my fields only or rest of the village's also", he asked.

"They have taken over all the fields."

This was one bit of good news. Avadesh Prasad owned half the acreage of Bijulia and the rest of the village owned the other half. If the naxalites had only taken his lands then he would have had to fight alone. But now the whole village was involved. He could now easily convert the fight into a caste war. The residents of Ramnagar were of the Bhumihar Brahmin caste while the residents of Bijulia were of the harijan community. It would be a fight between the Bhumihar's and the Harijan.

Avadesh Prasad disappeared into the mansion and came out after ten minutes holding a piece of paper. "Mahavir Lal," he ordered, "take the jeep and driver into the village and announce that I want all the villager's to assemble here in this courtyard within an hour."

"As you want master", replied Mahavir Lal as he and the driver rushed out.

"Jehangir, I would like a word with you?", ordered the zemindar.

Jehangir walked up the stairs to the verandah and was motioned by Avadesh to enter the living room. Jehangir walked in as Avadesh seated himself on the couch. "Sit down", he ordered.

Jehangir sat down cross legging himself on the ground.

"Jehangir are you a communist?".

The mahout sat silent.

"I know you are a communist. Why don't you speak up?"

"I am communist minded master, but I'm not a naxalite".

"You do have a soft corner for them?".

"No I don't".

"How come you are communist minded but are against the naxalites".

"Master, we live in a democratic country where people vote their representatives to power. If the communist party wants to reform the rural countryside, then it should go to the people and convince the people about the values of communism. It should try to get their votes and form a government. Then only will it be able to bring in reforms. The naxalites are extremists and a misguided lot. They are terrorists who aren't even behaving as one body. They are divided into several groups.

"Jehangir, try to put yourself in my shoes", asked the zemindar. "Imagine that you were the master of all this property and you are sympathetic with the poor and landless from deep in your heart".

Jehangir nodded.

"Tell me frankly, would you be able to distribute all this property amongst the poor, especially when an acre of land sells for ten thousand rupees, a horse costs thirty thousand and a jeep costs sixty thousand. Will you have the strength to give this all away?".

Jehangir was taken aback as he stuttered. "No master. I wouldn't be able to".

"Well that's my problem and my predicament, and

the problem and predicament of my class".

Jehangir nodded his head.

"What should I do. Give me a frank answer?".

"Fight for your right".

"And what is my right?"

"To protect your property and family".

"And where are you in this picture?"

"You saved my life. My life is yours".

"I mean in the fight, what will you do?".

"I will fight for you master".

Avadesh Prasad smiled and called Jehangir over to him. As the mahout walked up, the zemindar got up and hugged him. "Go and get the elephant, camels and horses and prepare them for the fight", he ordered.

Jehangir walked out of the mansion and taking hold of Malla Prasads trunk, he led the elephant to the Haathikhana. The two pehelwans followed him. "The two of you prepare the horses and camels while I prepare the elephant, "then turning to the elephant he ordered, "Chaiy".

Malla Prasad at once lowered his hind legs and fore legs and soon had his belly on the ground. A dirty mattress was lying in a corner of the "Haathikhana". Pulling the mattress over to the elephant, Jehangir hauled it onto the latter's back. Then taking a long rope he ordered the elephant to get up. Throwing the rope over the mattress to the other side, he went under the underbelly and fetched it back making a knot and pulling the rope tight, he threw it over the mattress to the other side a second time. He again fetched it and tied a knot. This act was repeated twice more till the mattress was tightly tied to the elephants back. "Now you are ready", Jehangir muttered as he walked out of the Haathikhana with his gun reassuringly slung from his shoulder.

The pehelwans and Jogi were brushing the horses. They later fitted straw cushions on the camels humps. The men heard a commotion in the courtyard in front of the mansion and realized that the villagers had assembled. Leaving their wards, the four humans went off to see what was happening.

"What's happening?", belched Glaxo.

"Don't know", replied Malla Prasad. "I just brought back three over exited humans from the river".

"Jehangir has put that mattress on your back, that means that you will be having quite a few people sitting on it".

'I don't know", replied Malla Prasad. "Ask the horses. They are the oldest around here, they should know?"

"There is a war on", neighed the horses. "There is going to be a battle".

"Who are they going to fight?", asked Malla Prasad.

"Humans who live on the other side of the river".

"You mean to say the humans will fight the humans?".

"Yes, and you will a part of it".

"Me a part of it?", Malla Prasad was surprised.

"Yes you will be a part of it. The humans will use you to instill fear on the other humans. There was a similar war a long time ago, before you came here. There was a fight and Paddum Prasad who is buried there, had a wail of a time throwing humans with his trunk and trampling down thatched roofs".

Malla Prasad cocked his head to the right and wondered. He could see the hump on the ground near the boundary wall. Feeling eerie he looked away. “Will they use those firesticks?”, he asked. He had seen Jehangir shoot down a vulture with his shotgun. The blast had frightened him.

“Yes”, replied the stallion, “They will be using the firesticks. When there is a fight, they always use them”.

“What about the bull’s will they also take part in the fighting?”

“They are too busy fighting amongst themselves over who owns which cow. They can do nothing but fertilize them. In a fight, they are the first ones to show their rumps and run away”.

“What did you say?, what did you say?”, belched Headache.

“They said we are useless?”, belched Rumpache.

“We are the first ones to run off in a fight”, mooed Neck ache.

“We’ll show you how manly we are”, they all belched in unison. “For a start ask the cows?”

“They are a bunch of useless louts”, mooed a cow.

“Who said that?”, belched Headache as he marched down the rows of cows,” who said that?”, he ordered and suddenly jumped as a roar erupted from the courtyard. “What was that?”, belched the terrified bull.

“The human’s are going to war”, neighed the horses.

My god a war”, belched Neckache, “where to hide?, where to hide?, tell me where to hide?”

“We told you”, mooed the cows, “those bulls are a bunch of lazy louts”.

Another roar erupted from the courtyard and Avadesh Prasad’s voice could be easily heard. “Gentlemen, friends, our lands and crops have been usurped by the Harijans of Bijulia. Do we accept this", he asked.

"No", roared back the crowd.

"We belong to the caste of the Bhumihar's. Bhumi-ka-haar. It means the caste which owns the land. If we don't fight back, then soon all our lands will be usurped and we will become Bhoomi-ka-heen. That is the caste without land. Do you accept this?"

"No", roared back the crowd.

"Are you prepared to fight for your caste dignity and your property?"

"Yes", the crowd hollered back.

"Are you willing to fight to death for what is right?"

"Yes", screamed back the crowd.

"Then prepare yourselves. The government machinery has proved unfit to fight the naxalite menace. It has been unable to protect the lives of the landlords, therefore we will have to take the law into our own hands. Tonight we will burn and destroy the village. All of you be prepared by evening. Muster up enough men, guns, horses and jeeps. I will pay three quarters of the expenses and the rest of you will have to pool in the remaining quarter. Tonight, do not be afraid to fight. We will deal with the government and the law courts later", then raising his clenched fists Avadesh yelled. "We will be victorious".

"Avadesh babu zindabad", roared the crowd.

"Wait", shouted Avadesh. "Remember to be back by evening and remember to avoid bloodshed. You will kill only if it is necessary".

"Can I speak master?", interrupted Jehangir.

"Speak", shouted back Avadesh.

"Let everyone assemble here at night. We will walk

five kilometres downstream and ford the river there. If we cross the river here, the naxalites will be alerted and they will be ready for us. If we ford the river downstream, then they won't understand what we are upto. We could attack them at early dawn when it is twilight. Then they won't know what hit them".

The crowd roared in applause.

"In your earlier life", Avadesh commented, "you must have been an army general".

The mahout bent down low as his right hand fell down to his thigh and swung up to his fore head in a salaam.

"You heard what Jehangir said?", shouted Avadesh. "Does anyone have a better idea?"

The crowd mumbled but no one replied.

"That's final", shouted Avadesh, "now everyone disperse and prepare for the fight, and send the boats five kilometres downstream".

Jehangir, Jogi and the two pehelwans walked towards the cow shed and their wards as the crowd dispersed.

"Wonderful", whinnied Rani, "Now well get a chance to get back at the humans".

"What do you mean by that?", asked Cadilla.

"Tomorrow I'm going to kick the human's in their bottom's."

The bull's gaped awestruck with their mouths wide open "Is she going bonkers?", asked Headache.

"Don't know", replied the cows who were also dumbstruck. "I don't think she knows what she is talking about."

"What are you all looking at me like that for?", asked the mare," I said that tomorrow I will be kicking the humans on their bottom's. Why are you all gaping at me? When I say that I will kick the human's, I will kick the human's."

"She's right", commented the stallion as the gaping bovines turned their horned heads to gape at him. "And those camels over there. Ranbaxy, Cadilla and Glaxo, they will all be doing the same. Malla over there will also be doing his bit."

"Are you all crazy," belched the bull. "Do you know what the humans have with them. 303 rifles, sten guns, Bren guns, Tommy guns, Sherman tanks, Paton tanks, Spitfires, Hurricanes, Messerchmitts, bazooka's, anti tank guns, and what do you horses have other than your hooves".

"And the camels have only humps", added Rumpache.

"It amounts to a Hara Kiri", continued Headache, "you animals are walking into a trap. You won't come back alive."

The mare looked at Malla Prasad and whinnied "You can see how brave these bull's are. They are already thinking of showing the enemy their rumps."

"Haw, haw, haw", belched the camels.

"Excuse me", trumpeted Malla Prasad, "I also did not understand what you meant by kicking the humans. Don't you think It's a wee bit dangerous, after all they have those firesticks which make horribly loud noises".

"He's right", belched Headache, "Jumbo's right, I agree with him".

"Heh , heh, heh", giggled the horses as they neighed. "It's your first experience Malla. What we mean is that we will be fighting with the humans against the humans. The humans who will be riding us will make us do the kicking".

"And you will be asked to throw some of them around with your trunk", added the stallion.

The tip of Malla Prasads trunk entered his mouth as a little child's forefinger enters his lips when he is deep in thought. He looked at Jehangir Khan who was sitting in a corner of the Haathikhana and wondered. Was it true that this human would ask him to throw around other humans? It was unthinkable.

Darkness soon took over after the sun slowly set and the villagers who were now armed to their teeth slowly trickled in. Some were on horses while most were on foot. Three jeeps roared in. They were overloaded with armed men who had with them an assortment of weapons which were either made by the local blacksmiths or were of world war I vintage. A few villager's proudly showed off their blunderbusses.

Avadesh Prasad came out of the mansion dressed in an expensive white dhoti and white kurta. He had a belt across his chest which was studded with red cartridges and in his right hand he held a double barrel shot gun. "Open the jeeps hood", he ordered the driver.

The driver and a few people unbuckled the buckles and pulled down the jeeps hoods and the little army waited till midnight after which they started their slow journey downstream following the banks of the Ganges.

The two horses trotted alongside Malla Prasad with the pehelwans sitting on them. Jehangir as usual was perched on the elephants neck proudly holding his double barrel shot gun and behind the elephant were the three camels each with people sitting uncomfortably on their humps. Jogi held one of the camels reigns and behind the animals were the foot soldiers and other horses and leading the cavalcade were the five jeeps which were overloaded with wildly exited gun toting men.

"So Malla", neighed the stallion, "you're going to have your first fight today."

"I still find it hard to accept that the humans will fight other humans", replied the elephant.

"I will kick like this and this", neighed the mare who had to be controlled by the pehalwan who pulled in her reigns in tight to stop her from kicking. "Whoa, cool it", he shouted.

"I still find it hard to accept the humans will fight other humans and kill them. Only ants behave like that. I have seen armies of them march on armies of other ants and they fight and kill each other".

"Well that's precisely What's going to happen", replied the stallion.

"The humans have no manners", spoke Ranbaxy. "Even in times of crisis they don't allow us to urinate on the ground. Look at the idiots who are walking alongside the three of us. They have fire sticks in one hand and bottles in the other. I haven't urinated on the ground since I was born".

"Neither have I", added Cadilla.

"Heh heh heh", giggled the mare as she gave another kick with her hindlegs.

"I feel sorry for those camels", rumbled Malla Prasad, "they are always surrounded with the men with bottles. It was the doctor who put them into that trouble. I wonder where he is just now".

Unknown to Malla Prasad, Gopesh Babu the village doctor was proudly sitting in the second Jeep with a trunkful of his twangy lotions which he had hurriedly concocted for the battle. He was adamant to save the lives of his caste brethren and was sure that his twangy lotions of this and that dipped in cows or camels urine and purified with cowdung, would be successful today. The proud doctor did not know that chaos reigned in the heavens. The almighty was overloaded with new arrivals and wanted some one to reverse the proud doctors jeep so that it went back to the village. Many lives would be spared then. The proud fellow sitting in the second jeep was virtually a time bomb.

The little army soon reached the rendezvous with the boats. One by one the jeeps used their four wheels to spin themselves up the ramps and into the boats which took them to the other side. The boats ferried the horses and the foot soldiers while the camels and elephant forded the river themselves.

The villagers of Bijulia hadn't expected the twilight attack. Some of them had got up at the sound of the roosters crowing and taking their lota's, they had gone to the fields to defecate. It was the people defecating in the fields to the south of the village, that saw the jeeps approaching with people firing from over their bonnets and wind shields. Just behind them were three camels, an elephant and a bunch of horses behind whom were the foot soldiers who were all madly firing in the air.

"Its an attack", shouted a villager as he left what he was doing and with a dirty bottom ran back towards the village.

"Run, run", shouted the others as they ran with their

bottoms still filthy. "The zemindar has attacked, forget your lota's and run".

"Elated at the sight of the running villager's the jeeps picked up speed with the camels and the other animals closely behind.

"How do you like it?", neighed the horses.

"Seems exiting", trumpeted Malla Prasad as he ran. Sitting on his neck, Jehangir was kicking into his ears to make him run faster. The mahout was exited and seeing the running defecators he lifted his shot gun and fired two shots in the air.

"Yahoo", neighed the stallion at the mare. "I bet I will kick more humans than you.

"Yippee", whinnied the mare, "if you do that, then I will owe you a months oats".

"It's a bet then".

"It's a bet".

The camels were also belching and grunting excitedly with some foot soldiers stubbornly running beside them with bottles in one hand while they fired their pistols in the air with the other.

The leading jeep with Avadesh Prasad sitting in the front seat approached the entrance of the village which was blocked by a few horse carts. "Ram them", ordered Avadesh.

The driver accelerated and the jeep crashed into the horse carts over turning some of them and smashing its own headlights in the process.

"Reverse and ram again", ordered Avadesh.

The jeep reversed as a hail of arrows hit the wind shield. The driver slammed the gear to forward and kicking up dust, the vehicle lurched forward and rammed into the overturned horse carts a second time.

Malla Prasad did not have to reverse. Jehangir kicked into his ears as he screamed "Agath" and Malla Prasad found himself bulldozing through a thatched hut with scared chickens flying in a flurry. The elephant understood now what the horses had meant and what Jehangir wanted. He lifted his trunk to look as horrible as possible and trumpeted, then lowered it and pulled down a thatched roof. He saw a few men throw down their bows and arrows which had been aimed at the jeeps, as they panicked and ran.

The camels with the bottle holding foot soldiers who were still close on their heels, had entered the lanes and by lanes and ran jauntily around as the people on their humps and bottle holders fired madly in the air.

The horses were galloping all over the village chasing woman and children and kicking with their hind legs. "Yahoo", neighed the mare as it gave a couple of kicks and sent two people flying into a thatched hut.

"Eeeh", whinnied the stallion as it sent a couple of turbaned men crashing through a thatched wall.

"That's two each".

"The mare kicked again", sending one more turbaned fellow flying into a coupe. "I'm three now", she whinnied. "One more than you".

The stallion bucked and kicked sending two more bare bodied turbaned figures flying into a pigsty.

"That's four to my credit, now I'm one above you".

The horse riders were having a hard time controlling their exited wards who had stopped galloping and were only kicking around.

The jeeps had ploughed through the horse carts and

were now roaring through the lanes and by lanes as their wheels spun and squashed fleeing chickens and lambs, while the people in them fired madly in the air.

Malla Prasad saw a bare backed turbaned man run. He ran forward and swung his trunk catching the mans right ankle. He swung the trunk into the air and sent the human flying into a double storied thatched hut. "Wheee", trumpeted the elephant, "this is fun". He swung his trunk again and hit a running man on the bottom and to his delight he saw the fellow fly through the air and fall into a water trough. "Pra-ra-ra", he trumpeted, "where are the horses?"

"Were having a terrific time", neighed the stallion.

Malla Prasad caught the hair of a man peeping out of a window. He was pulled out and flung into another window.

"Now I know what you meant by the humans fighting the humans", trumpeted Malla Prasad, "here take this and this." The elephant had repeatedly thwacked a hefty looking man on the bottom. "Hey that fellows got whiskers just like my master's", he squealed. Walking over to the man Malla Prasad swung his trunk and hit the man's calf's sending him sprawling to the ground. The person turned around and screamed when he saw the huge elephant towering over him. "Nooooo", he squealed.

Malla Prasads trunk travelled to the man's face and felt for the whiskers which twirled upto the ears. It caught hold of the hair and ripped it off. The trunk then travelled up to hand it over to Jehangir. It seemed as if the elephant was saying, "here take it and put it on".

"Are you enjoying yourself Malla", neighed the stallion.

"Terrific", trumpeted the elephant.

The camels were also having a belching time and were making full use of the chance to get back at the humans. They ran around biting some one here, someone there, someone on the nose, on the bottom or in the ear. "This is one hell of a way to live", belched Ranbaxy. "I wonder what Malla is doing". He did not realize that Glaxo had taken advantage of the commotion, and having shaken off the bottle holding humans, she was happily and rapidly urinating on the ground.

Realizing that Malla Prasad was wildly thwacking around and since this was precisely what Jehangir wanted, the mahout had stopped controlling him and was concentrating on loading and reloading his shot gun and firing in the air. It wasn't necessary to kill anyone since all the naxalites were on the run. There was chaos, but it was a one sided fight. From the start seeing all the people firing from the jeeps and the animals backs and not having any fire arms themselves, the villagers of Bijulia had panicked and run. The only piece of resistance they had put up was to barricade the villages entrance road with horse carts. This had been however smashed down by the jeeps .

"Hey what's this?", squealed Malla Prasad, "Someone is attacking me".

A bare bodied turbaned naxalite had gathered courage and had decided to fight back. He took a spear and aimed it at the elephant and charged. "Haiyaah", he screamed, "haiyaah".

"Now this is what I call sportsman spirit", squealed the elephant as it swung its trunk which hit the spear sending the weapon flying into a cow shed. The man spun around in two circles with the force of the thwack, and when he stopped, the trunk encircled the ankles and flung him up fifteen feet into the air. The man cart wheeled thrice before he landed in a haystack where he opened his eyes not sure whether he was alive or dead. "Am I alive", he asked himself loudly, "am I alive". Hearing the elephant trumpet, he looked up in time to see it hurl another person into the air. The fellow cart wheeled and fell head first straight into a well. The loud splash and the spurt of water told the naxalite that the person had had a happy landing.

"I'll get that elephant if that's the last thing I do", thought the naxalite who got up and hopped on to a an adjoining roof from where he jumped onto a cowsheds tiled roof. Jumping to the ground and startling the cows, he fetched his spear and aimed it at the elephant. "Haiyaah", he shouted, "haiyaah".

"Oh Don Quixote again", squealed Malla Prasad as he turned to face the man who was now charging with a spear.

"Haiyaah", the man shouted, "haiyaah."

"Get out of my way, you idiot", squealed the elephant as it caught hold of the spiked end and flung the spear into the air sending the naxalite cart wheeling into a trough.

"Ugh, from where did this human fall into our lunch?", mooed the cows. "Get out you dirty fellow". And two of the cows swung their horns into the naxalites bottom and sent him scurrying out of the cowshed. The spear followed suite and the naxalite was once again armed. “I’ll get that elephant if that’s the last thing I do. Turn around you idiot elephant”, the naxalite challenged. “I will kill you.”

Malla Prasad had just pulled down a thatched roof and was thwacking the inmates with his trunk sending them crashing out of the doors and windows when he heard the scream and turned around.

“Haiyaah”, the naxalite screamed, “haiyaah”.

“Oh no, Don Quixote again”.

“Charge”, the naxalite yelled as he ran eighty feet and spun around with the force of the thwack as his spear flew into the air. When he stopped, he was looking up at the great head. He put his fingers to his mouth and screamed.

Now what should I do to you, you stubborn fellow”, Malla Prasad rumbled, “should I tap you on the head like this?”

The trunk tapped the fellow on the head.

“Or on the arm like this.”

The trunk tapped the arm.

“Could you please turn around?”

The trunk turned the fellow around.

“OR SHOULD I SWAT YOU LIKE THIS”.

The trunk lifted and swung down sending the man flying into the cows lunch trough again.

“Ugh this person is stubborn, someone get him out of here”, belched a cow as it swung its horns at the mans bottom.

Further away the horses were having a hectic time as they kicked and counted. A lot was at stake. The mare would loose a months oats. “Whoa there whoa”, shouted the pehelwans as they tried to control their wards.

"One hundred and forty five", counted the stallion as a man went crashing to the ground.

"One hundred and twenty seven", said the mare as two people smashed into a closed door.

The horse galloped forward and seeing no one around, it entered an alley. It was followed closely by the mare. Seeing no one there also, the two galloped out and dashed straight into a group of running men who had guns and belonged to the zemindars army. Mistaking them for naxalites the stallion instantly turned around and three kicks sent three gunmen crashing into a hen house.

"Hold it, hold it", shouted the riders, "you are kicking our own men".

"You loose thirty points for that", neighed the mare, "ten points per wrong kick. Now you are down to a hundred and fifteen and I am one hundred and twenty seven".

Galloping forward, the two horses galloped down the road and seeing a bunch of fleeing men the stallion picked up speed and overtook them and soon eight of them were flying in different directions.

"One hundred and fifteen plus eight is how much?", asked the stallion.

"One hundred and twenty three. You're still five below me".

The foot soldiers on their part were a relieved lot. They did not have to kill anyone. The naxalites were on the run and from the outset they had won the battle. They had charged into the village running behind the jeeps, elephant and the other animals. Seeing the terrified naxalites on the run, they just helped them on. They butted them, kicked them, and pulled this fellow out of a thatched roof and another one from his house. They hardly had any work to do. The dirty work of terrifying the villagers was being done by the elephant.

Malla Prasad was running down the main road of the village with his bells tingling madly. No one seemed to be around. Accompanied with the horses and camels, the elephant ran to the end of the village. Coming out in the open the animals saw a line of humans running through the wheat fields in the distance. They were the naxalites who were running away.

A jeep drew up with a beaming Avadesh Prasad sitting in the front seat. He was happy because of the easy victory. "Fire some shots in the air", he shouted, "it will hasten them on their way".

The men raised their fire arms and fired in the air making an enormous din. "Okay", ordered Avadesh, "Search the houses. What ever you find, is yours and hurry, because I will soon torch this village".

Except for Jehangir, the men scampered off leaving the animals behind. They searched the empty huts and took whatever they could carry. They untied the cattle and loaded some of the goods onto them. Soon there was a line of people leading animals carrying assorted goods to the riverside where the boats were waiting. The village was torched and burnt down and Malla Prasad, the horses and the camels soon found themselves back in front of the cow shed.

"We had a wonderful time today", the camels commented. "After years of suppression, we got a chance to get back at the humans".

"They weren't the human's who suppressed you",

belched Neck ache. "They were other humans."

"They are all the same. All that matters is that they were humans, and I bit and kicked them at will", belched Ranbaxy.

"We should be thankful to our master who gave us this opportunity to let out our frustration", belched Cadilla.

"What did you all do?", asked the cows.

"Ask the horses", belched Ranbaxy, "who won the bet? They were racing each other on who could kick more humans".

"One thing is for sure", neighed the mare", I won't be able to sleep for quite a while now. I'll never forget the sight of me and Raja galloping gallantly through the village kicking any one we liked. Wow those humans bottom's were soft. Our strong hooves sent them crashing all over the place".

"But who won the bet?", asked Glaxo.

"It was a draw", replied the horses, "We kicked one hundred and twenty eight each".

"What?", belched Headache. "The two of you kicked two hundred and fifty six humans between you?"

"That's excluding the humans on our side we kicked and the points we lost for that".

"You mean to say you fought the sten guns", Headache interrupted. His eyes had become round balls in amazement. "You mean to say you fought the Bren guns, or Shermans or Paton's or Tigers".

"No", neighed the horses.

"You mean to say the humans did not use the Spitfires, or Hurricanes or Messerchmitts or Zeroes or bombers".

"No".

"You mean to say, you kicked the humans who are masters of all these machines with your hooves only?"

"Yep", replied the Stallion.

"Why is Malla Prasad silent?", asked Glaxo.

Everyone turned towards the elephant who was now mattress less. He was standing as though in a dream.

"So Malla, how was it today", asked Ranbaxy.

"I'm drunk", replied the elephant, "really drunk. I just did not expect to do all that I did today. Wow it was one hell of a fight. There must be more than fifty humans amongst the humans whose bones I broke".

"Did you enjoy it?".

"Enjoy it? Why I loved it. Imagine it, I have been in bondage since the day the wasp told me I would be a slave. And today was the first day I got back at the humans. Wow I did enjoy it. I sometimes feel like pinching myself to make sure I'm not dreaming".

"Anyway you did a good job", replied Glaxo

"I did a good job? Are you kidding. I went wild, I was wild, my master let me go wild".

"You know", neighed the horses", it was actually because of you we were victorious".

"How?".

"When the masters iron horse reversed and you dashed through that hut and trumpeted loudly. There were some people shooting arrows at the master. You were directly above them. They saw you, and by god you looked nasty. They left their bows and arrows and fled. Seeing them run, the rest of the naxalites ran without giving a fight, and soon everyone in the village were running."

"Here comes the master", neighed the stallion, "everyone keep quiet".

Zemindar Avadesh Prasad was walking in front of a large crowd. Shiela the maid servant was behind him and was carrying a tray of round yellow ladooes. Walking upto the elephant Avadesh held out a hand and stroked the trunk. "We are grateful to You Malla Prasad and you Jehangir. I in the name of the whole village am thanking you. Shiela give me the tray", he ordered.

The maidservant handed Avadesh Prasad the tray who held it out to the elephant. Malla Prasad squealed a thanks and took a trunk full of the sweat yellow balls and stuffed them into his mouth.

"It was a terrific day today", thought the elephant, "the humans are feeding me because I thwacked the other humans, they do behave like ants".

Animal Friends

Seasons passed and news spread that the naxalites had raided a police station and stolen some .303 rifles and some pistols. March ushered in a short spring, May blasted the countryside with its hot breath, July brought in the monsoon rains which brought relief to the Bihari's and November saw people readying themselves for the cold winter. Time flew and Malla Prasad experienced the departure of another friend. Ranbaxy slowly faded out of the world. He first grew thin and his ribs bulged. The doctor who doubled as a vet tried his best to save him. He gave the camel lotion after lotion as a frowning Avadesh Prasad looked on, but the camel grew thinner and weaker and one day he couldn't get up.

"This doctor is useless", exclaimed Avadesh Prasad as he watched the camel die. The village cobbler brought a bullock cart and with the help of Jehangir and Jogi and some villagers he hauled the dead body onto the cart and trundled it away to a field outside the village where he sheared the skin off the carcass which he left to be gouged by mangy dogs and pecked by hook beaked vultures.

The horses too had grown old and after a few more months Raja could not get up. On getting news of the stallions plight, the zemindar came to see for himself. He bent down and stroked the black maine. "He was a child hood friend of mine", he said, "I learnt to ride him when I was in school. My father had bought him in the Sonepur fair." Then getting up he walked out of the cowshed. "Jehangir", he said.

"Yes master".

"Don't let the horse suffer".

"Yes Master".

"Shoot it."

Jehangir gulped, then stuttered. "But master".

Avadesh Prasad was walking towards the verandah of his mansion and without looking back he ordered, "Don't let it suffer, shoot it and bury it near Paddum Prasad. Don't let the dogs or vultures defile it".

The mahout turned pale as he turned around to look at the old horse and realized what Avadesh meant. What he saw wasn't the strong sturdy proud stallion he knew, but an old sad looking dying piece of flesh. It seemed that every minute of life it lived was a disgrace to that sturdy horse called Raja.

Jehangir felt for his gun. He realized it wasn't on his back so he went and fetched it from the Haathikhana. Taking it he walked out of the Haathikhana and stopped. He turned around and looked up into the elephant's eyes. It seemed to blink. Then turning around he walked upto the cow shed to where the stallion was lying. Uncocking the gun he pulled out a red cartridge from his belt and inserted it in the slot in the barrel. He cocked the weapon and looked down at the head. The eye was shut. Aiming the barrel below the ear, and at point blank range, Jehangir looked away and fired. Something warm hit his leg. Looking down he realized it was blood. The horse was lying still.

Jehangir walked out and shouted to Jogi who was already running towards the cowshed. He had heard the loud bang and wondered what had happened. "Go get a spade and dig a ditch deep enough to bury the horse", ordered the mahout, "dig near the elephants grave".

"You shot the horse?".

"Yes".

Jogi's jaw drooped as he entered the cow shed. He saw the dead horse and knelt for a second near the head. There was a red hole behind the ear. Getting up, he went to a corner of the shed where he kept the spade. Picking it up he walked out towards the little mud hill next to the boundary wall and started digging. He soon had a seven feet deep rectangular ditch dug. Going back to the mansion he called the two pehelwans who helped him trundle the bullock cart to the shed where the four humans pulled and heaved the dead horse onto the cart. The bullock cart was trundled to where the ditch was and with the help of bamboo stakes the four people pushed the dead body out of the cart and onto the ground. They then got together and pushed the body into the ditch. The legs did not fit in so Jogi climbed down and bent the knees so that they were in line with the underbelly. After he climbed out the four got together and shovelled the mud back in. Soon there were two little mud hills against the wall.

Malla Prasad looked at his bald friend and wondered, "Why did he shoot the horse? Why did he do it?". It was becoming increasingly hard to understand the humans and their behaviour.

"Why did he do it?", the elephant squealed.

"I don't know", neighed back the mare.

"The humans are unfathomable", mooed the cows,

"they sometimes love you, and when you are going to die, they use their firesticks on you."

"Disgusting", belched the bulls.

"I fail to understand them", belched Glaxo, "look at those four people with the bottles. Don't they feel dirty collecting my urine. They follow me where ever I go."

"I haven't urinated on the ground since I was born", complained Cadilla.

"Why don't you kick them?", advised a disgusted Malla Prasad.

"My god no", replied Glaxo, "I don't want to attract their anger."

That night it was an unhappy animal world that went to sleep. They all dreamt of the smart black stallion that was once their friend. They were ill at ease. If the humans could use the fire stick on the horse, then the firestick could be used on them also. Jehangir did not realize that his little act of mercy had been misunderstood by his and Jogi's wards.

The seasons however flowed and soon the animals forgot the tragedy and resumed their normal lives. The bulls swore to chew off the cows ears if they winked at the elephant, the mare was now the wisest in the cowshed, Malla Prasad went as usual to his sugar cane field to bring back the cane, and the grass which was hacked off was given to the two camels to chew. As usual the animals wondered at the curious ways of the humans.

"Look here comes the fat mistress", trumpeted Malla Prasad as he raised his trunk as though in a salute. He liked the fat mistress, not because she was fat, but because of the sweet round yellow laddooe's she gave him to eat.

"Look Shiela", the mistress squealed in delight, "Malla Prasad is saluting and wishing me."

The mistress hobbled upto the elephant and ordered the maidservant to give her the prayer tray. As usual she took the tray and showing it to the elephant she dipped her thumb into the red vermilion powder and drew a red line on the elephant's forehead who was now seated in front of her with Jehangir holding the rope which encircled his neck. Time had taken its toll on her too and she was a wee bit fatter, and looked a wee bit older.

Lighting the little lamp on the tray she proceeded to twirl it in circles in front of the elephant's forehead singing "Jaya Jagdisha Harrey."

"Stop croaking you fat pumpkin", rumbled the elephant "and pass the yellow balls."

"Look Shiela", squealed the mistress as she continued twirling the tray, "look he is blessing me, Jaya Jagadisha Harre."

"Pass the laddooe's, you fat slob."

"Oooh Shiela he's blessing me."

Malla Prasad waited for the tray twirling to stop which he knew would be followed by laddoe eating. However today she twirled the tray for a longer period of time. Stopping, she handed the tray back to Shiela and folded her hands in prayer. "My lord", she prayed, "I have been married for the last seventeen years, but till today I am barren. The villager's have started secretly calling more a raven." The mistress stopped and looked at the elephant. She was pleased to see that it was looking at her." The learned doctor has been treating me for the last fifteen years", she continued, "and yesterday he told me to pray to you and ask you for a child. Your holiness, I beseech you to please listen to my prayer. I have been faithful to you for the last fifteen years. Please, I beg you please let me conceive a child." Then remembering she added, "make it a boy child."

"Give me the round ball's", the elephant squealed.

"Your holiness please fill my barren womb."

"You want me to fill your womb", rumbled Malla Prasad "Rani you heard that?"

"Your holiness, put your trunk on my head and bless me."

"Rani you heard that?"

"What", neighed back the mare.

"The mistress wants me to fertilize her."

"Please your holiness", begged the mistress. "Please bless me with a boy child. The doctor told me that if you blessed me, I will conceive."

"Now madam", rumbled the elephant, "this is preposterous, impossible."

"What is she saying", neighed the mare.

"She wants me to fill her belly with a boy child."

"I told you", neighed the mare, "these humans are unfathomable. You don't know what they will ask next."

"Glaxo is there a solution to my problem", Malla asked "after all you're a female also."

"None", belched Glaxo," ask the cows, they will know better?"

There were seventy five horned heads peeping out of the cow shed. "Relax", they mooed. "It's the Hindu habit of praying to animals. They ask us for all sorts of things. They come to us, tinkle their bells and twirl their prayer trays and ask us to make their businesses more profitable, or to pass them in their school or college examinations, or help them get a job. You see they think we are a goddess."

"Then what should I do?" asked Malla Prasad.

"Just nod your head, and you will get the result."

Malla Prasad nodded his head.

"Oooh Shiela look", squealed the mistress. "Lord Ganesh is nodding his head.

"Nod more", mooed the cows.

Malla Prasad nodded again.

The mistress clapped her hands in delight. "Oooh Shiela. His holiness is nodding his head, he is saying yes."

"Yes madam", squealed the exited Shiela. "Its a miracle."

The doctor was correct", said the mistress. "He was the one who told me to request his holiness the elephant."

"Keep on nodding your head", advised the cows.

Malla Prasad went on nodding his head.

"Eeeeh", squealed the mistress. "He nodded again. Shiela, I feel like dancing. The heavens have opened up, the stars are smiling on me. I know I will conceive."

Jehangir looked at his ward. He was perplexed at the way it was nodding its head. "Was it really a God", he thought.

"Okay now you got your baby, so hand over the yellow balls", rumbled Malla Prasad.

"Look Shiela he is blessing me with words, give me the laddooe's."

"Yes that's it", rumbled the elephant.

The mistress held out the tray and the elephant

hurriedly picked up the balls with its trunk and dumped them into its mouth. “Delicious”, he squealed.

“Oh the heavens”, the mistress was looking up as if she had already conceived. “Shiela, hurry lets give the good news to the master.”

The fat lady turned around. The rump looked huge but Malla Prasad did not thwack it. He knew that his trunk was heavy and strong now, and if he did thwack her, he would easily break her bones, so he quietly watched her waddle off toward’s the mansion closely followed by the faithful Shiela. “There she goes”, rumbled Malla, “Now how am I supposed to put a boy child in her womb? And why a boy child only and not a girl child.” Turning to the camel he asked, “Glaxo what is the difference between a male and a female child?”

“I don’t know.”

“Do you know Rani?”

“I don’t know”, replied the mare, “but what I do know is that the humans prefer a boy child to a girl child.”

“But why?”

“I told you before”, belched Glaxo, “the ways of the human’s are unfathomable. It is hard to say what they will say or do next. It did not make any difference to me when Cadilla here was born.”

“We’ll explain”, mooed the cows. “Do you ask god for things that you want?”

“Yes”, replied Malla.

“The human’s regard us god’s, that’s why they come and ask us for various items, though some may sound weird.”

“I understand that”, rumbled Malla, “but why the preference for a boy child to a girl child?”

preference for a boy child to a girl child?"

"Don't know", replied the cows, "but one thing we are grateful to the almighty is for making us the possessions of the Hindu humans."

"Why", asked Cadilla.

"The Hindus pray to us. They say we are a goddess, so our lives are safe. If we belonged to a Muslim human we would have been hacked and devoured by now. The Christians also like eating our meat, and call it beef. Our brothers in England and America say that they are born and bread to be finally strung up from meat hooks, so if our master's act weirdly, we our happy, at least our lives are safe."

"You've go a point there", belched Glaxo.

"That goes for you two camels also", mooed a long horned Hariyanvi cow, "the people who relish our meat, relish camels meat too."

The camels gave s shudder.

"Do they eat elephants meat?", asked Malla Prasad.

"Mostly no."

"Then we should be grateful that the humans behave weirdly", belched Glaxo, "and pray to you and use your dung to purify their homes, and pray to Malla Prasad there."

"Yes", belched the animals together, "we should be grateful that the humans behave weirdly."

"And lets pray to the almighty", belched the bulls, "that they continue behaving weirdly."

"Yes", belched the rest in unison.

It was a grateful bunch of animals that retired for the night, happy that the humans behaved weirdly. Malla Prasad went to sleep in his Haathikhana, the cows and the mare slept in the shed, the camels slept they were tied, and Jehangir slept on a cot near the elephant with his torch reassuringly beside him.

As the animals dreamed, a slithering rope slithered across the fields which faced the Mansions double lioned gates. It wasn't frightened at the sight of the two cement lions and slithered on. It had the stamp of spectacles on its head and was two and a half feet long. It was a cobra and had just emerged from a rat hole it had annexed and was enjoying the fresh air. It slithered on into the mansions courtyard and turned right towards the cow shed. Passing some of the cows it turned left towards the sleeping camels. Seeing the outstretched legs of the sleeping Glaxo, it mistook them for logs or sticks so it proceeded to slither over them. It slithered safely over her hind legs, but as it was crossing in between the two forelegs, Glaxo woke up and seeing the snake half across its lower fore leg, she panicked, belched, and tried to get up. The snake got stuck between the legs, and being of a short temper, it turned and bit the camel in the thigh. Glaxo felt the pain and belching madly she sat up as the snake slithered on. Hearing the desperate belches, Jehangir and Malla Prasad opened their yes. Jehangir shon his torch and the beam fell on the slithering rope. (In Bihar, a snake is not called a snake during the nights, but a rope. There is a strong superstition that it will attack in the dark and bite if it is called a snake.) Seeing the cobra slither off, Jehangir realized that the world had lost the camel called Glaxo.

The next day, the animals had their heads drooped low as their dear Glaxo was carted away. Her death reminded them of the black stallions departure and they felt extra gloomy. Cadilla now was alone since the other camels had died. Jehangir and Jogi had sat they felt extra gloomy. Cadilla now was alone since the other camels had died. Jehangir and Jogi had sat the whole night beside the dead camel with their heads in their hands. They despaired at the successive loss of their animals. Cadilla had her head drooped and Malla Prasad consoled her. "Don't worry Cadilla", he rumbled "we are with you."

"I know", replied Cadilla, "but she was my mother."

"We grieve with you Cadilla", rumbled Malla, "but by god I won't let anyone snatch you away from us."

"How can you do that", belched Headache.

"I'll prove it."

Malla Prasad got the chance to prove his promise that same day. It was a hot afternoon and the snake that had bit Glaxo was returning from where ever it had been to, and Cadilla saw it slithering towards her through the harvested wheat fields which were directly in front of her. Cadilla belched and attracted Malla Prasads attention.

The elephant trumpeted out loud and lunged forward, but was stopped by the rope tying its huge feet to the stakes in the ground. "Pull back Cadilla", he squealed, "pull back."

Cadilla belched and pulled at the tether that tied her to the wooden stake.

The cobra had lifted its hood and had climbed the fields mud boundary and was now on the flat ground directly in front of the camel.

"Go back", squealed Malla Prasad, as he pulled at the ropes that tied him to the stakes.

Not having ear's, the cobra did not hear the elephant's order and went on slithering towards the camel who was now madly belching and tugging at heaved as the snake closed in on Cadilla.

"Pull hard", repeated the elephant when suddenly the rope tying him to the stake snapped. The elephant shot forward and running upto the reptile he brought his right forefoot down on the creatures head and pressed down hard. The tail squirmed and lashed till it finally stopped. Removing the foot and turning around, the elephant lumbered back to where he had been standing in the Haathikhana and waited for Jehangir to come and tie his feet again. He had proved that he wouldn't allow anyone to snatch Cadilla from him.

I Want A Spouse

Malla Prasad now realized that he was living in a land where superstitions and unscientific beliefs ruled the human mind. The elephant had started feeling lonely and wanted a partner of its own. Of its own kind. He desired a female elephant, a wife, a spouse. He noticed that all the animals that lived around him were of both genders. Male and female, and they loved each other and gave birth to little one's. Of course the bulls were a pain to the cow's. The cows however gave birth to beautiful little calf's. Glaxo had given birth to Ranbaxy and Cadilla. Malla Prasad had been surprised when he saw the little camels coming out of Glaxo's rear.

"Even the mangy dog has a mangy bitch to keep him happy", complained Malla Prasad.

"But I'm also alone", belched Cadilla. "I'm happy".

"I know, I know", replied the elephant. "But I want a spouse, a female elephant with a trunk and huge feet like mine. Some one I can call my own".

"But aren't we your own?", replied Cadilla.

"Were not made for each other", replied Malla Prasad, "though I do like your company."

"Then why groan?", replied Cadilla.

"Look dear I feel nasty. I want a spouse, I feel like hurting someone."

Not suspecting anything wrong, Headache was coming back after grazing on the green grass which had sprouted up near the hand pump. He had his eyes on his harem and was passing the Haathikhana when the elephant walked three feet forward, lifted its trunk and swung it down and with a loud "thwack", it hit the bull on the rump. The impact caused the bull to go crashing to the ground.

"Ouch that hurt", belched the bovine.

The elephant lifted its trunk and swung it down a second time, as the bull tried to get up, and thwacking it, he sent it sprawling back into the ground in a cloud of dust.

"Yeeow, that hurt", belched the bull.

"Get out of there", belched Neckache, "get out of there, it seems Jumbo is on heat".

Malla Prasad lifted his trunk up and trumpeted loudly. Taking advantage of the interval, the Bull gathered itself and limped off to a safe distance. "Awe, that hurt", he belched. "My rump hurts".

"Serves you right", belched Cadilla. "Didn't you see he was irritated, he was on heat?"

"On heat?", groaned the bull. "What's on heat?".

"He wants a spouse you dope, and at such times he becomes nasty and only his bald keeper can control him. Sometimes he also fails".

"Then why didn't you tell us that before".

"Hark what do I hear?", belched Cadilla.

"Its the sound of an iron horse approaching", replied the mare.

"It seems the master is returning from the city", suggested Rumpache.

"The mangy dogs told me that the mistresses stomach had ballooned into a huge round half ball", neighed the mare, "they suspect that she was pregnant and might give birth to a cub or a calf. What do the humans call their little one's?".

"Don't know", replied Hoofache.

"Anyway I think she is returning".

The sound of the cars engine drew upto the mansion where it stopped. There was a roar and shouts of "long live Avadesh Babu, long live the mistress", and, "long live the little child".

"What is it", belched Hornache, "now what are the humans screaming about".

He looked towards where the car was parked and saw Jogi and Jehangir rush towards the cowshed, pass them, and run to the elephant.

Malla Prasad had his trunk above his head and was trumpeting loudly. "Shut up Malla", shouted Jehangir, "and bring down your trunk".

Malla Prasad looked down at his bald friend. "Now what is it?", he trumpeted.

"Shut up", ordered Jehangir as he waved his hand for the trunk. The trunk came down and the tip was soon in the Mahouts hands.

"Watch out", belched Headache, "I've just got two solid thwacks on my bottom. The fellow is on heat".

Holding the trunk Jehangir caressed it while the bare backed Jogi rubbed the huge thighs. "Stay quiet", whispered Jehangir, "the mistress has given birth to a baby boy. She claims that it was you who fertilized her".

"I don't care about the mistress or who fertilized her", squealed the elephant, "All I care is I want a spouse. Give me a spouse".

"Shut up", Jehangir scolded as he picked up the little spiked spear and poked a thigh. "Shut up or I'll give you a few more pokes. The master and mistress are coming".

The elephant fell silent as its little eyes fell on a red and white object passing the cow shed. The figures were blurred and since elephants are short sighted Malla Prasad squinted his eyes. The mistress was wearing a bright red sari, looked much thinner then the last time he had seen her, and the master had a broad grin on his face. The mistress had a little bundle in her arms at whom she occasionally "coochi cooed".

"Please stop", said the priest as he tinkled a little bell at a cows rump and mumbled something.

The master and mistress turned towards the Haathikhana and closely followed by the learned doctor and the priest and the two pehelwans and the faithful Shiela carrying the tray of laddooes, the little group walked upto where the elephant and the two humans stood.

Seeing the master and mistress approach, Jehangir bent down low and swung his hand from his thigh to his head uttering the words "salaam alaikum. May god bless the child".

"Thank you Jehangir", the master replied, "but we must thank his holiness for fertilizing the mistress."

"Now what did you say sir?", the elephant rumbled, "I never fertilized her. I swear I never touched her."

The priest walked upto the elephant and tinkled a little bell. Tinkle, tinkle, tinkle, it tinkled as he recited some Sanskrit verses. The elephant looked down at the little group perplexed. "Look I don't know what you fellows want?", it sqealed, "but all I ask from you is a spouse. An elephant spouse".

Tinkle, tinkle, tinkle, tinkled the bell as the priest went on with his mumbo Jumbo which even the humans could not understand.

"Look", rumbled the elephant "Give me a spouse, a wife, with a trunk and a tail and huge legs like mine".

Tinkle, tinkle, tinkle and the humans folded their hands and bowed in obeisance.

"Look, all my nerves are taught. I'm controlling myself because of this bald friend here. I think I'm going mad".

The humans had finished their silent prayer and were now looking up at the elephant with beaming faces.

"Look all of you I'm finding it hard to control myself, please go away".

The mistress held up her little boy child so that the elephant could see it. "Thank you your holiness".

"Thank yourself".

"It was your blessings that fertilized her", spoke Avadesh Prasad with folded hands.

"You planted the seed in my womb", spoke the mistress.

"I did not plant any seed in any womb", then turning to Cadilla he squealed. "You heard that Cadilla. The mistress says that I planted the seed in her womb".

"Haw, haw, haw", belched the bulls, "haw, haw, haw Jumbo's in a fix".

"Haw, haw, haw", belched Cadilla.

"I didn't know the humans could be so dumb", belched Headache, "even a blind man can see the two aren't made for each other.

"Shut up", belched Cadilla, "You're talking vulgar".

"I thank Gopesh Babu here who advised me to ask

you for your blessings", continued the mistress, "finally it was your blessings that made me conceive".

"Cadilla, you heard that?, she says it was my blessings that made her conceive".

"Play the game, Malla play the game", advised Cadilla, "and you will get those delicious round balls".

"The mistress turned to her husband and motioned to the learned doctor. Avadesh Prasad fished out a wad of notes from his kurta pocket and handed it to the learned gentleman who bowed low as he accepted it. The zemindar did not know that it was his wife's heavy build and inner strength to fight his twangy medicines which had kept her alive as she drank his lotions for the last fifteen years. The almighty had been ill at ease when ever she drank his concoction fearing her soul would come flying up any moment, and was relieved each time it didn't.

The mistress motioned to the two pehelwans and Jogi, and the zemindar handed them some money each. The priest also received a fat wad. The mistress finally looked at Jehangir and the zemindar filled the mahouts right kurta pocket with currency notes.

The priest lifted his bell and tinkled it as he mumbled some mumbo Jumbo when the mistress interrupted. "I have been praying to his holiness all these days, punditjee, so let me do so today".

Handing over the child to the zemindar the mistress took the prayer tray with the little lamp in it, and motioned to Jehangir to bring the elephant down.

"Chaiy", ordered the mahout, "Malla chaiy".

The elephant hesitantly but obediently came down on his knees and the mistress dipped her thumb into the red vermilion powder in the tray and drew a red line on the elephants forehead".

"There's the teeka", commented a beaming zemindar.

The mistress then started her usual ritual of twirling the tray in front of the elephants head, who cocked it sideways to look at Cadilla. "What should I do now?", he asked.

"Play the game".

"How?".

"Ask the cows".

Malla Prasad looked towards the seventy five horned heads peeping out of the cow shed.

"What should I do?", he rumbled.

"It seems you forgot", mooed the cows, "nod your head and see the result".

The mistress was singing "Jai Jagadesha Harrey" in her croaked voice as she twirled the tray.

Malla Prasad nodded his head.

The humans were surprised.

"Oooh Shiela", squealed the mistress, "Lord Ganesh is nodding his head".

"Now what to do?", rumbled the elephant.

"Continue nodding", directed the cows.

Malla Prasad went on nodding his head. The humans were delighted. The zemindars beaming face shone more, the smiling pundit tinkled his bell louder and the pehelwans and learned doctor were standing with folded hands and bowed heads, deep in desperate prayer. Jehangir Khan the Muslim mahout was in deep thought. He did not believe in elephant gods but swore he would convert to Hinduism if someone gave a scientific explanation to this unique phenomenon. Why the elephant nodded its head when ever the fat mistress twirled the tray in front of him?

"Keep on nodding", mooed the cows.

Malla Prasad went on nodding.

"Ooh Shiela", the mistress squealed as she handed back the tray to the pundit and was clapping her hands in delight. "His holiness is blessing me. I think I will get another child. Give me the laddooes".

The maid servant handed the tray to the mistress with the laddooes piled up in a neat little pile. Holding out the tray she smiled at the elephant who proceeded to take the round yellow balls into its trunk.

"Madam you shouldn't be outside the mansion for too long", warned Jehangir. "It is hot and the boundary wall is very low. Anyone could jump over it. It seems the master has forgotten about the naxalites".

"Oh yes", remembered the fat mistress as she put down the tray and turned to take her child. "I forgot about the naxalites".

"I forgot too", mumbled Avadesh Prasad.

"Jehangir", the mistress ordered. "We are going so it is your duty to feed the laddooes to his holiness".

The little group turned around and Malla was faced with three rumps. The zemindar's one which peeped through the thin fabric of his expensive dhoti, the fat mistresses one which was draped in a red sari, and the pandits skinny one which was draped in a saffron dhoti. Malla lifted his trunk but stopped. Jehangir was desperately holding on to it as the little group walked towards the mansion followed by the waddling mistress.

"How about eating some of the laddooes", suggested Jogi after the little group disappeared into the mansion.

"The mistress told us to feed the elephant", replied Jehangir, "I will not steal from him."

Jogi dipped his hands into the yellow pile and pulled out two round balls which he proceeded to stuff into his mouth. "Thank you Malla Prasad", he said through a stuffed mouth, "thank you for the laddooes".

Jehangir got up and walked into the Haathikhana. Collecting the rope he threw it onto the elephants back. Picking up the dhow and gun, he slung the gun from his back and taking the elephants trunk he walked out into the afternoon sunshine. The elephant resisted and mumbled and Jehangir understood. It wanted the laddooes at which Jogi was greedily gouging.

"I think you've stollen enough", commented Jehangir as he picked up the laddooes and put them in a piece of cloth and slung it over his shoulder. Taking the little spear, he climbed up the trunk and perched himself on the neck. Jabbing at the ear, he "agathed", his ward forward and soon the grumbling animal and the unsuspecting mahout were on their way to the banks of the great river and the sugar cane field. The elephant rumbled from deep inside its belly. "I want a spouse", it said, "don't you understand I want a wife. An elephant wife".

"I wish I understood your language", Jehangir spoke to the elephant, "I wish I understood your language".

"I want a spouse, a wife", the elephant rumbled.

The two soon reached the cane field, and leaving the elephant behind, Jehangir went and hacked a huge bundle of sugar cane. Bringing the elephant up, he ordered it to sit after which he loaded the cane on the back and tied a rope tightly around the belly and the sugar cane.

"Maiy Malla", he ordered after he had climbed onto the neck. The elephant got up and automatically started walking towards the village but stopped after covering half the distance. Jehangir kicked into the ear to make it move forward. "Agath", he ordered, "Agath".

The animal refused to move and instead gave out low rumbling noises from deep in its belly.

"Agath, agath", ordered Jehangir as his toe continued nudging behind the elephants ear. The elephant did not respond but violently shook its head. It was then that Jehangir realized that his ward was on heat.

"Agath", he shouted as he took the spiked spear and jabbed at the skull. The elephant squealed. Jehangir went on jabbing at the head as he went on shouting "Agath".

"I want a wife you idiot", squealed the elephant and to Jehangir's surprise, it started running". "I want an elephant wife".

"Ruk, ruk", shouted Jehangir as he caught hold of both the ears and pulled back. This was to make the elephant stop. It was moving too fast and the bobbing back was causing the loosely tied cane to fall off.

"I won't", squealed the elephant. "I want a wife".

Jehangir pulled back hard at the ears. More than half of the cane had slipped off the back.

"Don't pull my ears", squealed the elephant as it ran forward swinging its trunk as it did so.

Most of the sugar cane had fallen off and Jehangir lost his temper. Taking the spear he jabbed at the head and hurt the pachyderm as he repeatedly screamed "Ruk, ruk, ruk".

"I hate you humans", squealed the elephant. "I hate you humans who kiss your wives behind closed doors and deny me a wife".

The elephant did not realize that it was a victim of a weird belief that prevailed amongst the mahouts and elephant owners of Bihar, that a bull elephant should not be exposed to a female one. If it was, then it would refuse to leave the female. It would go out of control and follow the female where ever she went. It was equivalent to losing ownership of the elephant. To regain control of the pachyderm, the owner would have to buy a female one and incur the expenses of maintaining the two huge beasts, therefore it was better to keep the male single and a female outer sight if you wanted to keep only one male elephant.

Jehangir realized that his ward had gone out of control, and the two were fast approaching the entrance of the village so he attempted to stop it a last time by catching hold of both the ears and pulling back.

"I hate you", squealed the elephant as it swung its trunk up in a circle and hit Jehangir with such force that the mahout fell back and found himself lying face skywards on the bobbing back. Losing balance he turned towards the right and slid off the back and fell with a thud on the ground as the elephant rushed on. "Serves you right, for keeping me spouseless", it squealed.

The elephant was now without a mahout and was racing at full speed towards the village squealing and trumpeting as it did so. "I'll teach you humans who kiss your wives behind closed doors, I'll teach you to keep me spouseless", squealed the elephant as it dashed through a thatched hut and smashed it down as though it was made of paper.

Seeing the elephant smash through the hut, the villagers scampered off in different directions. The raging elephant looked nasty so they ran as fast as possible into brick houses. "Don't run you selfish louts", Malla Prasad squealed, "come back and face me".

The elephant lifted its trunk and chased some men into an alley. It was close to one short fellow whose dhoti had opened, so it swung its trunk sending the fellow crashing through a door. "Serves you right", squealed the elephant.

Word spread through the village that zemindar Avadesh Prasad's elephant had gone berserk and was rampaging through the lanes and by lanes so people locked themselves up in pucca houses and peeped out of window slits.

"Where are the humans?", squealed the elephant as it barged down a road, "there's no one around, okay then take this". The elephant pulled down a tiled roof. There was no one inside.

"And take this".

It pulled down another tiled roof.

"And this".

It crashed through a mud house.

"And this".

It smashed down a hut and ran through the learned Doctors dispensary. The learned quacks patient was lying on a cot with an open mouth for the doctor to pour the twangy lotion in. The angels in heaven sighed in relief as Malla Prasad barged in and the patient and the learned doctor scampered off. That was one soul less the learned doctor would throw up. "The elephant has gone mad", shouted the humans from roof tops. "Where is Jehangir?"

Jehangir was running at full speed towards the Haathikhana where Cadilla was tied. Reaching the cow shed he ran towards the camel. He knew he couldn't control the elephant and at the moment no man in the world could. There was one animal whom he suspected would be able to control the elephant. He had a hunch. He had seen the elephant confront the camel a couple of times in what seemed to be a quarrel. Cadilla would give a sort of low hiss which would send Malla Prasad scurrying back to the Haathikhana. It was a hunch and Jehangir decided to try it.

As he approached the camel, he realized that she was tugging at her tether and it seemed that she knew her friend had gone berserk and only she could control him. Running over to her Jehangir opened the tether and the camel was off running in her jaunty motion towards where the mad trumpeting was coming from.

Jehangir also ran madly trying to keep pace with the camel as she rounded bends and entered thin alleys to run towards where her friend was pulling down a roof. People on roof tops who saw the camel run madly past them and cursed the zemindar for letting his mad beasts go free. "Where is Jehangir?", they shouted at each other and saw the mahout running full speed after the camel.

Turning a bend the camel was suddenly face to face with the elephant who was pulling down a roof. She stopped and for a few seconds stood still. Jehangir rounded the bend and stopped. Walking a few steps back he took the shot gun from his shoulder and loaded it and waited. He and a few window peepers saw what happened.

"Why did you come here?", squealed the elephant.

"To take you back", belched the camel.

"Go back or I'll hurt you".

"No, you won't".

"They won't give me a spouse".

"Come back with me".

"I won't, I want a spouse".

"This is no way to ask for a wife."

"I want a female elephant."

The camel lifted its head and walked forward and caught the elephant's right ear in her teeth. The nasty look on the pachyderms face disappeared and the elephant looked childish as it cocked its head to the left as a child does when his teacher catches hold of the ear. Then in front of the amazed roof top on lookers the camel led the elephant down the road all the way to the Haathikhana and didn't leave the ear till her friend was standing in the spot where he usually stood near the stakes. Turning around, she walked back to where she was usually tied and waited for Jehangir to come.

The mahout however had got a fright and it took him two hours to gather the courage to go and tie the ropes around the huge legs. He slowly approached his old friend and finally managed to tie the feet. As he did so Malla Prasad rumbled,

"Sorry dear Cadilla,
you are their saviour.
Of the humans I have a grouse
they refuse me a beautiful spouse".

For The People, By The People, Off The People

A group of people who were all wearing white dhoti's and kurtas in assorted stages of dirt walked into the courtyard towards the verandah. Seeing the zemindar seated in an arm chair, they folded their hands and namastayed him. They had a portly looking priest in tow who had a little bronze prayer tray in his left hand.

"Yes, what is it?", asked the zemindar.

"Sir, we have come to request you to lend us a cow"

"Why, is someone dying?"

"Yes", replied the person who had the glummest face of all. "My father is breathing his last. The learned doctors medicines could not save him, therefore we need a cow".

"Jehangir", shouted Avadesh to the mahout who was standing near the tractor. "Go and send Jogi to me".

Jehangir was soon back with the bare backed Jogi.

"What is it master?".

"Go with this group to the cowshed and let them choose a cow. They can borrow it for the day".

Thanking the zemindar, the little group followed Jogi to the cowshed where they chose a black Hariyanvi cow which looked more Indian. The Jersey and the Frezian cows had foreign looks on their faces and did not fit the Hindu concept of a mother cow, so after they had made their choice, the priest walked over to it and stood in front of the great horns. Tinkling the bell with his left hand, he twirled the tray clockwise in front of the bovines face mumbling some mumbo Jumbo as he did so.

After the priest finished tinkling the bell, one of the glum faced people took hold of the tether and led the cow out of the cowshed while the others trailed behind and the priest regained tinkling his bell and mumbled his prayer. The group followed the cow to the courtyard, thanked the zemindar, namastayed him and walked out of the double lioned gates just as a group of men in white clothes holding little flags and with little white caps on their heads walked in. They stopped and faced each other and the politicians expressed their condolences at the expected departure of the elderly gentleman's soul.

"But please give us your votes", they added, "We are your caste and you must help us keep our community in power".

The glum faced people walked on while the politicians walked upto the verandah and started zindabading the zemindar.

Back in the cow shed the cows were telling each other how lucky the Hariyanvi cow was and wished they had been chosen instead. Rani understood what they were speaking off but Cadilla and Malla Prasad were surprised.

"Did those people buy the cow from the master?", asked Cadilla.

"No", replied the cows, "they borrowed her for a day".

Headache had stopped grazing near the hand pump and was lumbering back to the cow shed. Approaching the Haathikhana he stopped. He remembered the pain in his bottom where the elephant had thwacked him and did not want to risk getting another shot.

"Hey Jumbo", he belched, "are you okay today?".

Malla Prasad looked at him and laughed and said, "Stop and gently pass".

"Are you okay today?".

"I'm okay".

"No heat?"

"No heat".

The bull slowly lumbered on keeping a suspicious eye on the elephant and only when he was a couple of trunk lengths away did he turn his face and trot upto the cowshed to inspect his harem. Finding one cow missing he belched, "Where did she go?, where did my Buttercup go?"

"She was taken away by the humans", replied Cadilla.

"What?, my beautiful Buttercup was sold?".

"No", replied the cows, "he was borrowed for a day".

"By whom?".

"Some people came with a priest who rang his bell in front of Buttercup after which they led her away".

"Oh, so she's gone to lead a human soul to heaven. Its alright, she will come back soon".

"Excuse me Headache", interrupted Cadilla, "you just said something peculiar. Could you repeat it?"

"What?".

"The thing you said about leading the soul to heaven".

"Oh that", belched the bull, "there's nothing special about it. Its part of our daily life. You see the humans think that my harem are mother goddesses and have the power to lead the soul to heaven. When a human is about to die, it is believed that a cows tail can lead his soul to heaven".

"That's peculiar".

"Its interesting", squealed Malla Prasad.

"Occasionally when the learned doctors learned medicine fails, which most of the times it does, and a villager is about to die", continued Headache, "the humans who don't have a cow come here and borrow one. They come and tinkle a bell and twirl a tray over the head and lead the cow away who is made to turn his rump towards the dying human. The dying person is made to hold the tail after which it is regarded that the cow has led the soul to heaven".

"Now that is ridiculous", replied Cadilla.

"Impossible", said the elephant.

"Well whether it is ridiculous or impossible it doesn't matter as long as we live. You see the cow which is taken for the tail holding ceremony is fed Guava's, Apple's and other fruits and you all know that it is the humans respect for in us that we are alive or we would have passed through their digestive systems long ago as beef".

The bull suddenly jumped and scampered of as a loud roar erupted from the verandah as people screamed "Avadesh Prasad zindabad".

"What was that?", belched the alarmed bull. "Are the martians attacking?".

"Avadesh Prasad zindabad", roared the humans.

"Wheeeee", squealed the elephant causing the bull to jump again and scamper back to the shed. "What's wrong with Jumbo?. Is he on heat again?".

"Pra-ra-ra", trumpeted Malla Prasad, "for the

people, by the people, off the people".

"Now what was that for?", belched Cadilla.

"Pra-ra-ra, I'm going to thwack humans again, squealed the elephant as he swung his trunk in a circle, "like this, and this, he swung the trunk again. "And like this. I'll send the humans flying all over the place".

Headache gawked at the elephant. "Its worse than his heat", he grumbled. "Jumbo's gone bonkers".

"I'll swing my trunk like this", Malla Prasad swung his trunk in a circle, "And send the humans flying like that".

"All you animals do you hear", belched Headache, "Jumbo's gone bonkers so no one go anywhere near him, he even wants to thwack the mighty humans in open warfare".

"I'll use my huge feet to squash them", squealed the elephant.

"But they have AWACS", replied Headache.

I'll squash them like ants.

"But they have Stealth fighters and Jaguars and Spitfires and Messerchmitts".

"I'll send them flying through the air like this".

"But they have ground to ground missiles, Harpoons, Scud's, Scud busters or Patriots and what do you have other than a long trunk and four huge falarial feet".

"Shut up", belched Cadilla, "he's not so dumb as you think. Even I think I will be biting a few humans".

"My god, you too?".

"And me also", neighed Rani . "If Malla there thwacks the humans and Cadilla bites them, then there is no reason why I won't be giving a few of them a taste of my hooves".

"I strongly think we bovines are the only sane animals around here", belched Headache.

The bull did not know what Malla Prasad and Cadilla meant. The humans had used the camels, elephant and horses to scare the naxalites in the Bijulia fight. They had given the animals a free hand to fight the naxalites in whatever way it had suited them as they themselves fired in the air. The same animals on another occasion had been sent in a booth capturing mission during the last elections. In Bihar, election time is war time when people of different castes align with different political parties and campaign for their caste members. Theoretically people go and cast their votes to choose their representatives. Practically most people stay back in the safety of their homes as the various candidates and political parties go on a rampage. Overnight petty criminals are in full demand and roadside Romeo's become generals and strategists. Maps are drawn up of the different areas, their population and their caste. Horse trading becomes rampant and wine and money flow. On D. Day (election day) the different cast armies become active and the modus operandi is simple. The areas which are dominated by ones own cast are strongly protected and the people are helped to cast as much votes as possible, but the areas dominated by other caste groups with different political affiliations are disturbed. This is done by exploding bombs, shooting, murdering and creating a fear psychosis so that the public in that area do not venture out to vote. The more adventurous ones go in and steal the votes. They stamp the ballot papers in favour of their candidates and pay the presiding officer to accept it as authentic. This precisely is called booth capturing.

The animals however did not understand all this. They just enjoyed the free hand they were given to deal with the opposing humans. This was the reason why the animals had got exited. They had relished the two occasions in which they had been allowed to kick and bite and thwack the humans and Malla Prasad had recognized the slogan shouting that was taking place in the courtyard. "For the people, by the people, off the people". It was amongst such slogan shouting that he had gone into the attack in the last elections.

"Hah here they come", he squealed as Jehangir led a group of men upto him. They were carrying a battery, a mike and a loudspeaker and were shouting, "for the people, by the people, off the people".

"Chaiy Malla Chaiy", Jehangir ordered and the elephant obediently sat down. The mattress was taken from the corner of the Haathikhana and hauled across the elephants back after which a saffron bed sheet was draped over the mattress. Malla Prasad got up and the rope was sent four times across the bed-sheet and under the belly and tied. Another rope travelled around the neck and across the mattress to pass under the tail and travel back to the neck where a strong knot was tied. The politicians climbed onto the back and Jogi handed over the battery to one of the gentlemen.

The loudspeaker was pulled up and Jehangir climbed onto the neck and nudged the ears ordering the elephant to get up. "Maiy, Malla , Maiy", he ordered.

The elephant got up and walked majestically out of

the Haathikhana with the people sitting on its back. They held little orange flags in their hands with a rose printed on it. It was their candidates election symbol. He was a member of the Bhumihar caste and his name was Jagadev Prasad. His opponent was a harijan and the latter had the backing of the backward castes and some of the naxalite groups.

Malla Prasad walked past Cadilla and some one got a bright idea. "Why not take the camel along?"

It was a good idea so Jogi was called and a politician threw down a saffron sheet and flag to him. The cow herd hurriedly made Cadilla sit down and draped the hump with the sheet as he himself climbed on. Kicking at the shoulder blade he made her stand and waited for the elephant to pass after which he made the camel fall in line behind. Holding the flag in one hand and the reigns in the other, he followed behind the elephant.

"Look how smart he looks", drooled a cow.

"Majestic", mooed another.

"Robust", mooed a third.

"Strong", belched a fourth.

"INSECT", belched the bull, "shut up and put your heads back in", he ordered, "you're not supposed to be looking at other males other than me".

"Male chauvinist pig", belched a cow.

"Who said that?", belched Headache as he lumbered down the line of cows. "Who said that?"

There was no reply.

The elephant and camel walked out of the double lioned gate and turned left to enter the village. A politician took the mike in his hands while another made the necessary wire connections.

"Jagdev Babu zindabad", the politician yelled into the mike.

"Zindabad, zindabad", the others yelled back.

"Jagdev babu zindabad", he continued.

"Zindabad, zindabad", the rest went on.

Malla Prasad was made to stop at the village square. It was a confluence of four dirt roads which led to different parts of the village, and was surrounded by little pucca houses.

"Ladies and gentlemen", shouted the mike holding politician. "Please pay attention. We are the supporters of Jagdev Babu who is an independent candidate. His symbol is the rose, the rose that symbolizes everything that is beautiful in life. Prosperity and a good livelihood for all. We are of the Bhumihar caste, the same caste which you belong to".

People were seen rushing towards the square and soon a little crowd had surrounded the animals.

"Ladies and gentlemen", the politician continued, "times have changed. Our state has been divided into two distinct groups, the backwards and the forwards. The Harijans and Sudra's that form the backwards two major blocks have sunk their differences to join hands and fight us. They want to rule this state. For centuries we Brahmins were the rulers of this land and our fathers and fore fathers were the masters of the sudra. The sudra was our slave and worked for us. They have however raised their heads under the symbol of the goat and threaten to overturn us. They want to come to power and vote in a sudra government. Is this acceptable to us?".

"No", yelled the crowd.

"Today they are under one banner and they want

to overtake our lands. They will form the government and pass laws that will snatch our property. Would you like this?".

"No", yelled the onlookers.

"Jagdev Babu is an important member of our caste. He is rich and landed like the rest of you and understands the woes of the farmers. He has got the strength and the will to fight for our community and is ready to give his life for our cause. The backwards have rallied behind their candidate 'Jugal Mochi', who is a harijan by caste and is adamant to snatch the property of the Brahmins. It is therefore left to you to decide on whether you want to live as a pauper or a slave or whether you want to live as your proud selves. As master of your own property and master of the sudra. I therefore request you all to think carefully and not to waste your votes. Jagdev Prasad is the best bet for our cast, and he is the only one from this community who can fight for our rights. You must also remember that members of some naxalite groups are backing the backward candidate and this could prove a bad omen. I would therefore request you citizens to get together and as a whole body vote for him, so lets shout together, "JAGDEV PRASAD ZINDABAD".

"Jagdev Prasad Zindabad", the crowd yelled back.

"Jagdev Prasad will win".

"Jagdev Prasad will win", the crowd shouted back.

Five kilometres away in a little village another group of villagers had assembled in the village square to listen to a group of politicians speak. They were of the backward caste.

"Ladies and gentlemen, we are not here to ask you

for your votes only. We are here to ask you to strengthen yourselves and your community. We are called Sudras and Harijans and are treated insolently by the upper caste Brahmins. I would like to remind you that we have been treated as slaves for generations and our fathers and forefathers had been tortured by them. They toiled for the Brahmins making them richer. We were weak and they were unified. They snatched our lands and became richer. I would like to ask you, is this to continue?".

"No", yelled back the crowd.

Today things are not the same . Put together we Sudra's outnumber the forwards. According to the latest government census, seventy percent of the population of this state are backwards and fifteen percent are forwards. This fifteen percent want to rule us by promising us pittances like free education and jobs. All this is secondary. What we want is equality with them and our share of the landed property. We will not wait for them to give as doles as aid. We will take what is ours. For years the Brahmins have been the rulers. Since independence and before that they have been the educated elite. On the basis of our support they have ruled the land. If we have the power to vote a Brahmin to rule the state then why don't we vote one from ourselves to power. We want a sudra, a man born from a sudra woman's womb to rule Bihar".

"Zindabad", screamed the crowd, "three cheers for Jugal Mochi".

"Now listen friends, we do not have time for more speeches in this village as we have to cover more villages whose residents are waiting for us. So now what I have to say is very important. The forward casts will be building up gangs of marauders who will come and try to terrify you and snatch your votes. Make sure that every one of you, men and women, go and caste your votes. Remember, the goat is our symbol and be ready to ward off the people who may come to snatch your votes".

"What about us", replied a villager. "If they can make gangs to snatch our votes, why can't we do the same. We could raid their villages and snatch their votes".

The politician straightened his white cap. "We have our own gangs", he said. "They will go on the rampage on election day. Moreover we have got the backing of some of the naxalite groups. We will also snatch votes".

As the politician walked over to a waiting Jeep, Malla Prasad and Cadilla entered another village where the politicians gave the same fiery speeches asking their caste brethren to vote for them.

"Are you enjoying it", Malla Prasad asked Cadilla.

"There seems to be a lot of excitement around".

"Just like the last time".

"But tell me Cadilla, if the humans have to choose their representative, then why do they fight amongst themselves?"

"I don't know, but what I suspect is that they do not agree on the same man, that's why they squabble and fight".

"Remember the villages we raided the last time. We aren't visiting them and those people on my back seem to avoid them".

"They have every reason to. Those villages belong to the other group, and if we go there, those humans will lynch the humans sitting on us. They might even use their fire sticks on us".

Malla Prasad shuddered. "Its Good that we are avoiding those villages", he remarked.

The animals were led back to Ramnagar after a long hectic day of campaigning and Cadilla was tied to her stake while Malla Prasad was taken to the Haathikhana. The politicians zindabaded Avadesh Prasad and left and returned early the next morning. The mattress with the saffron bed-sheet was re-tied to the back of the elephant, and this time Rani the mare joined the two animals and the little troupe went from village to village as the men on their backs shouted fiery slogans which aroused the excitement and sentiments of the villagers. "We are with you", the people shouted back. "Don't worry about our votes. Think of ways of capturing the Sudra's votes".

"Don't worry we have our plans", shouted back the politicians who were sitting on the elephants back. "We will capture their votes on election day".

The little group travelled from one village to another campaigning for Jagdev Prasad.

"Let's go to Punaichak", ordered a politician.

"We can't", replied Jehangir. "To go there we will have to cross a sudra village. They might get nasty".

"Let's take the risk, we might give them a speech or two also".

"It's dangerous", replied Jehangir, "those people hate us". "Are you scared Jehangir?"

"No".

"Then lets go".

"If anything untoward happens then I am not to blame".

"We'll take the responsibility", replied the politicians.

Jehangir turned his ward towards the village that hated the zemindar and his caste and his party. In the last elections, Malla Prasad had been made to rampage through the village. The villager's had fled and the people on Malla Prasad's back had jumped down and stormed the polling booth and stamped all the ballot papers in favour of their candidate. The presiding officer had been given a wad of notes to sign on the papers stating that everything had gone through peacefully and according to schedule.

Approaching the village Malla Prasad realized that a group of humans were standing in a line across the road with their hands behind their backs. They were blocking the villages entrance so he stopped.

"Why are you blocking the road?", asked a politician who spoke through the loud speaker.

"We won't allow you and those animals to enter our village", shouted back a villager.

"Why not?".

"We don't like your speeches".

"You should listen to every one's speech, the constitution says that".

"Yes and the constitution also advises you to send your wild elephant rampaging through our village".

"The last time it was different people dealing with you".

"We don't care who you people are, we will not allow that elephant and that flag to enter our village".

"Then we will enter by force".

"Don't try that".

"Jehangir, take the elephant forward", ordered the

politician.

"It is dangerous", whispered Jehangir.

"TAKE THE ELEPHANT FORWARD".

Jehangir gave a gentle kick at the base of the ear saying "Agath", and the elephant moved forward.

"Marro salle ko", shouted a person who was in the line which blocked the road. "Throw stones at them".

Suddenly all the men standing across the road had stones in their hands which they hurled at the elephant. The missiles flew through the air and hit Malla Prasad and the politicians. Bending down low and ducking the missiles, Jehangir shouted, "I told you this would be dangerous".

"Turn the elephant back, turn it back fast", shouted the politicians as they were repeatedly hit by the missiles, "lets get out of here fast".

That was however not to be. Cadilla belched and obeying her riders order she and Rani were soon galloping across the fields. Malla Prasad however was made of different mettle. The stone throwing was enough to instigate him and he rushed forward with his upraised trunk to wallop the stone throwers who seeing him had scampered off into the adjoining fields. Malla Prasad chased the people who had entered the field to his right, so the people who had run to the left stopped, turned and gave chase throwing stones at the men on top of the elephant.

"Turn him around Jehangir", shouted a politician, "turn him around".

"I can't", shouted Jehangir as he pulled back at the ears, at the same time trying to duck the flying missiles that were aimed at him. "He is angry and is out of my control".

The elephant realized that it was being attacked from the rear, so it turned around and chased the stone throwers. The people who were running away stopped and turned around and were now chasing the trumpeting elephant throwing stones at it. “Marro salle ko”, they shouted, “throw stones at the elephant.

A missile hit a politician on the jaw and the impact threw him back on the mattress. His legs shot up and he somersaulted backwards falling off the elephant to the ground, while the politician holding the loudspeaker lost balance on the bobbing back and slid off the mattress and fell with a clang on the ground. The rest of the politicians desperately held onto the ropes while the elephant chased the people who were taking turns at stoning him.

“Every one lay on your stomachs”, shouted Jehangir “and hold onto the ropes”.

The elephant had turned around and passing the fallen politicians it chased the people who were throwing stones at it from behind. Seeing the elephant turn, the stone throwers scampered off and the people who had been previously running, turned and gave chase throwing stones as they shouted and yelled. “Some of them surrounded the fallen politicians and abusing the latter they rained blows on them. They kicked, boxed and pulled the latter’s hair.

“Please spare us”, shouted the politicians, “please spare us”.

They were however spared only when the beaters saw the elephant turn and start chasing the people who were stoning it from the back. The stoners were now running towards them with the squealing elephant hot on their heals, so they scampered off.

"Stop", cried the battered politicians, "stop for gods sake stop".

This was however impossible as Malla Prasad was not in Jehangir's control. "Stop you humans", he squealed, "stop and face me".

The humans running before the elephant however had no intention of stopping and Malla Prasad realized that he was again being pelted from the back so he turned around and gave chase. The people who were throwing stones and beating the already beaten politicians scampered off while the people running off again stopped and gave chase.

"This is too much", squealed Malla Prasad as he stopped. The people running away also stopped. They had now grown tired and were scared. They didn't realize that their see-saw game of chasing, pelting, running and chasing the elephant had at last managed to scare the beast.

"These people are too cunning and dangerous", squealed Malla Prasad. "I think I should get out of here".

Giving a parting squeal the elephant turned and ran across the harvested fields as it occasionally lifted its trunk and trumpeted something or the other.

"Come back, come back", screamed a bruised politician, "come back for gods sake don't leave us here".

The other politician saw the loudspeaker and limped to it and taking the thin end to his mouth he blared, "COME BACK JEHANGIR OR WE'LL BE KILLED".

Jehangir and the remaining politicians were desperately holding onto the ropes of the mattress on the bobbing back and were in no position to stop the fleeing elephant. They heard the shouted pleas and the one blared through the loudspeaker and could not even sympathies. It was every man for himself. By not listening to Jehangir's advice, the politicians had poked their fingers in a hornets nest and had been properly bitten.

Malla Prasad ran all the way past the various villages and stopped only when it sighted its masters double lioned gate. Jehangir climbed down and taking the trunk started rubbing it to calm his ward. The remaining three politicians jumped off and refused to climb back on. They had got a fright and did not want another ride so the four humans led the beast back to the double lioned gate. Jehangir led Malla Prasad back to the Haathikhana where he tied the huge feet with ropes to the stakes. He then went off to see what was happening in the mansions verandah. He wanted to tell the master his part of the story.

Malla Prasad looked at Cadilla who seemed to be smiling. "You can't win always can you Malla?", she said.

"The elephant shook his head".

"How did you like it Jumbo?" It was Headache and he had got the whole story from Rani. "I told you not to meddle with the humans. I had told you, didn't I?"

"Will you shut up", Malla Prasad squealed.

"You said that you would thwack them on their rumps", continued Headache, "then what happened?".

"Look I can't help it if the humans make me fight the humans". Malla Prasad was now on the defensive.

"Sticks and stones did break my mighty bones, didn't they Malla?".

"Shut up will you".

"You'll send the humans flying over the roof tops won't you Malla?"

"Shut up".

"You said you'd squash them under your falarial feet, then what happened?", continuing his teasing Headache laughed, "and you came back running with your tail between your legs, is that so?"

This was too much and Malla Prasad got his chance to get back at the bulls. Neckache had been grazing on the green grass which perennially sprouted around the hand pump. Having eaten his full he was lumbering back towards the cowshed, and not knowing that Headache had teased the elephant, he was lumbering past Malla Prasad. Walking two steps forward, the elephant lifted its trunk and slammed it down on the bulls rump sending it crashing to the ground. The first thing Neckache thought through the pain in his rump was that the elephant was on heat. He got up and was thrown back onto the ground from a second shot.

"My god I better get out of here", Neckache belched as he got up and limped off. Seeing Neckache go crashing to the ground, Headache did his famous disappearing act. He scampered to the mansion and went around the corner from where he peeped back.

"I can't help it if the humans fight the humans", squealed Malla Prasad.

"Calm down, calm down", belched Cadilla, "We will get our chance, you can take you're revenge on them".

It was in the evening that the two politicians who had been left behind were brought back. On hearing the story the zemindar had sent some villagers in his jeeps who reached the spot and saw the two politicians doing kneel downs in front of the captors. Their clothes were torn as they were badly bruised and they had their hands to their ears as they sat down and stood up again. The new comers had fired in the air to disperse the crowd, and had collected the two politicians and brought them back.

"You shouldn't have been so rash", scolded the zemindar as he saw them off. They were going to the learned doctor for treatment. "You could have killed yourselves".

For the rest of the campaign the politicians of both the sides were careful not to cross into alien territory, and they campaigned only where they thought it was safe.

"For The People, By The People, Off The People" Part II

D Day came and everyone was full of excitement. The mattress was tied over Malla Prasad's back and three men holding guns and wearing gun belts climbed onto the elephants back. Jogi took the reigns of the camel and shared the hump with another gunman while one of the pehelwans rode Rani. As Malla Prasad walked past the cowshed, the cows fell head over heels for him.

"Look at him carrying those men with firesticks", drooled a short horned cow.

"Isn't he smart", drooled another.

"Look at his handsome face and trunk".

"Look how gracefully he sways".

"He's majestic".

"Smart".

"Robust".

"Strong"

Headache was nowhere around to snub his harem. The commotion and preparation for the fight had frightened him, so he had done his famous disappearing act and was peeping from the corner of the mansion.

Malla found himself facing the mansion and the zemindar and was standing in a row of animals. There were some horses from the village with armed riders on their backs, himself, Cadilla and Rani. Behind the row of animals were five Jeeps overflowing with armed men.

"Today is your chance to fight for your cast", the zemindar shouted, "make sure that the backwards do not cast their votes. Protect your own voters, shoot in the air and try your best to avoid bloodshed, but if it is necessary a couple of lives may be taken and if possible capture some booths for us. Now go".

"Avadesh Prasad zindabad", Jehangir shouted.

"Avadesh Prasad zindabad", the crowd shouted back.

"Jagdev Prasad zindabad", Jehangir shouted.

"Jagdev Prasad zindabad", the crowd yelled back.

Jehangir pulled Malla Prasad's left ear and the elephant turned towards the left in a half circle. "Agathing", and digging his toes into the base of the ears, Jehangir made Malla Prasad walk out of the gates and into the adjoining fields. The elephant, camel and horses travelled through the fields while the jeeps kicked up dust along the dirt road.

Entering a village dominated by the Bhoomihar caste, the little army was enthusiastically greeted. On asking how the polling was going on, they were told that every male and female in the village who was eligible to vote had been lined up.

"I think this is a chance to get your revenge", belched Cadilla.

"I think so", rumbled Malla Prasad.

The cavalcade carried on to the next village and realized that the polling was going on smoothly so they carried on to the third village where they were met by exited villagers who informed them that a group of marauders had raided the next village and was not allowing the villagers to vote.

"For The People, By The People, Off The People" Part II

"Come on Malla", belched Cadilla, "things are warning up".

Malla Prasad lifted his trunk and trumpeted as he ran. The animals with their riders dashed across the fields with the men excitedly shooting in the air.

"Run faster Malla", belched Cadilla.

"Come on", winnied the mare.

Malla Prasad picked up speed and was soon abreast the running camel and galloping horses. Together they dashed across the fields with the gunmen sitting on Malla Prasad's back desperately holding on to the ropes which tied the mattress to the back.

The animals soon approached the village and Cadilla was the first one to gallop in closely followed by Malla Prasad and the horses. Reaching the polling booth Jehangir pulled back the ears causing the elephant to slow down and stop. The gunmen jumped down and ran into the square little white coloured, tiled roofed house that housed the polling booth. They realized that all the ballot papers had been forcefully stamped and locked in the iron ballot box.

"They came in firing their guns", complained the villager's who had run up, "they fired at us and made us run away".

"It's hotting up Malla", belched Cadilla.

"Where did they go?", asked Jehangir.

"They ran off towards the north".

Jehangir nudged the elephants ear and made him walk upto the little cottage. There were two ballot boxes on a table which were locked and sealed.

"They stamped the ballot papers with the goat stamp and have locked and sealed the ballot boxes", complained the villagers.

"Aren't there any more ballot papers", asked a gunman.

"None".

"What nice boxes they are", thought the elephant as it let its trunk enter a window and fondled the boxes.

Seeing the trunk over the box Jehangir got an idea. "Utha Malla utha", he ordered.

"What did you say?", squealed the elephant.

"Utha Malla utha ".

"You want me to pick up the iron box?".

Jehangir nudged the ear as he repeated, "utha Malla utha".

Malla Prasad drew closer to the window and taking the box, he pulled back and sent the trunk with the box upto his master squealing, "here take it".

"Don't give it to me", Jehangir replied as he pulled the right ear and led the elephant to a nearby well. "Throw it down", he ordered and kicked a ear.

The elephant let go off the box which splashed into the water and slowly sank. Jehangir was about to turn him around when two gunmen ran up with the other ballot box and threw it into the well and watched it slowly sink. Satisfied that the ink stamp on the papers would blur and the paper would become mushy, and would tear if touched, the gunmen caught hold of the elephants tail and climbed onto its back.

"Where did those booth captures go", asked Jehangir.

"To the north", the villagers replied, "We suspect they were naxalites.

"But they had only bows and arrows", replied Jehangir. "You could have tackled them".

"They had guns. Police rifles and revolvers".

“For The People, By The People, Off The People” Part II

This piece of news alarmed Jehangir. Till now he knew that the naxalites were armed with spears and axes and bows and arrows, while the zemindar’s men had proper rifles and double barrel shot guns and pistols. The news the villagers had just given had an ominous meaning. There could be a shoot out, and human lives could be lost.

Turning the elephant around, he made him lumber down the road which led out of the village from where he turned north. Malla Prasad was again running.” Come on Cadilla”, he squealed, “come and follow me”.

The camel shot off after the elephant, closely followed by the horses. Soon she was abreast Malla prasad and added her belching to Malla Prasad’s squeals. “Isn’t it glamorous?”, the camel belched, “Dashing like this into battle”.

“I wish this could happen daily”, squealed Malla Prasad.

“Yahoo”, neighed the horses, “for the people, by the people, off the people”.

“Run faster Malla”, Cadilla belched as she got a thwack on her rump from her rider to run faster. “Pick up speed, I can see the village now”.

Malla Prasad picked up speed, but his lumbering body could not catch up with the camel. She was soon ahead of him with the horses galloping abreast him.

“Yippee”, neighed the mare, “for the people, by the people, off the people”.

“Yahoo”, neighed a stallion, “kick the people, bite the people, throw the people”.

“Eeyah”, neighed another and soon the animals were approaching the village with Cadilla well on the lead.

Inside the village the villagers who were all of the sudra community and were bare backed with only little loin cloth's covering their naked selves, were standing in line in front of the polling booth which was in a tiled roofed cottage. They were all putting the stamp on the symbol of the goat when they saw the camel swoop in closely followed by the barging elephant with the riders on his back firing madly in the air.

Cadilla dashed in lowering her neck to bite at a fleeing human. She nearly ripped off the ear.

"Run", screamed the villagers as they scampered off in different directions. "Run, the zemindars mad animals have come".

Malla Prasad was lucky as a person by mistake ran in the opposite direction straight towards him. At the last moment the man stopped, shrieked and turned away. His attempt to run was futile as Malla Prasad caught his right leg and pulled him back. "Aieee", the man screamed as Malla Prasad swung his trunk up sending the man flying into a thatched house. It had been quite a long time since he had thrown a human like that, so running forward, he swung his trunk at a fleeing figure sending him shooting on his way smack into a hay stack.

"Wheeee", squealed Malla as he threw another person who cart-wheeled in the air and fell on the roof of the polling booth. "How are you Cadilla, are you enjoying the for the people, by the people and off the people".

Cadilla was running around biting some one here and some one there, while Rani was busy kicking at different people. She made contact with some and sent them flying into thatched walls or chicken coupes or into troughs full of hay.

The gunmen on Malla Prasad's back jumped off the trumpeting elephant and firing in the air they dashed into the polling booth. One of them had his gun pointed at the terrified presiding officers head while the others hastily stamped the rose symbol on the ballot papers, folded them and put them into the little slit in the iron box. Soon all the papers were stamped and the ballot boxes were sealed with the presiding officers signature who signed to save his own life and for the little wad of notes he received from the gun men. Rushing out, they triumphantly fired in the air and shouted to Jehangir to bring Malla Prasad over. This was however impossible as the elephant was thoroughly enjoying the fight and was pulling down thatched roofs when it felt something poke its rump. A man was trying to poke a spear into his bottom. He turned around to face the impertinent fellow when he recognized the half naked dark turbaned person.

"Oh Don Quixote again", squealed Malla.

"Haiyaah", the man screamed as he attempted a second time, "Haiyaah".

"Get out of my way", squealed Malla as his trunk caught the attacking spear and swung it to the right, sending the man flying through the air onto a thatched roof. The fellow fell through the roof and shot out of the entrance door with two squealing women with brooms hot on his heels. They had just prepared lunch and naxalite had fallen smack onto it.

"Well get you", squealed the women, but seeing the elephant they turned and ran back to the safety of their huts, so Don Quixote had another attempt. He picked up the spear mumbling. "I'll get that elephant if that's the last thing. I'll do". Running straight for the huge animal who was facing the opposite direction and was pulling down another roof, he poked the spear into the thick skinned rump all the while screaming "Haiyaah".

"Oh no not Don Quixote again", rumbled Malla Prasad as he turned around and taking the fellow by his loin cloth he threw him into the air towards where Rani and the other horses were kicking. Rani connected perfectly and sent Quixote flying back in the air to fall in front of Cadilla who nipped him in the ear. His valiant scream of "Haiyaah", turned to a terrified, "Aieeeh", as he ran down the road with the camel in hot pursuit who was adamant to give him another nip.

Running after Quixote, Cadilla felt natures call and stopped to accompli. She looked around and saw no one with bottles around and realized that this was the first chance in her life to urinate on the ground so she let go and was surprised to see seven doors flung open and bare backed sudra's scamper over with their bottles to collect the medicine. They all had apologetic grins on their faces as they told Jogi, "You robbed our votes at least let us take the urine". They then squabbled amongst themselves to collect the potent liquid. Cadilla realized that the learned doctors sphere of influence covered this part of the countryside also. No wonder they said that he had a roaring practice.

Back near the polling booth the gunmen had run upto the elephant and holding the tail they had climbed up the huge feet to the back. Seating themselves they ordered Jehangir to head for the next village which was another sudra village whose votes they would snatch, so Jehangir turned the elephant around and made him run down the road past a standing Cadilla who had a bunch of dark skinned, bare backed humans squabbling under her urinating self. "Come on Cadilla", Malla squealed, "come on we're going to the next village".

"Come on Jogi", shouted the gunman who was sharing the hump with the cow herd, "lets not get left behind".

Jogi pulled the reigns as a bunch of horses galloped past him in a flurry of dust and Cadilla was soon in hot pursuit with Jogi and the gunman bouncing on her hump.

"I'm coming", belched Cadilla as she ran.

"Yahoo", neighed the mares as they ran.

"For the people, by the people, off the people", whinnied a stallion.

"Kick the people, throw the people, bite the people", belched Cadilla.

"Wheeee", squealed Malla Prasad as he turned right and dashed through the fields with the other animals hot on his heels. The men sitting on their backs were thoroughly enjoying the run. It looked like a victory run with all the animals gallantly dashing through the countryside with the men on their backs firing in the air. It was just like in the films they had seen in the sleazy cinema halls that dotted the countryside. The men were in high spirits and were adamant to rob a few more villages votes and then go back victorious to the zemindar who would most probably give them a fat baksheesh each.

"How many people did you kick", squealed Malla Prasad.

"Twenty four", replied Rani.

"And how much did you bite Cadilla?".

"I don't know".

"Yippee", squealed a mare.

"Yahoo", neighed a stallion.

"For the people, by the people, off the people", belched Cadilla.

"Hit the people, throw the people, kick the people", trumpeted Malla Prasad.

A village soon came into a view and Malla Prasad squealed in delight. "I'm going to throw more humans around".

"Yahoo", neighed the horses", we'll kick them on their bottoms".

"I'll bite all of them", belched Cadilla as she picked up speed as Jogi kicked into her shoulder blade to make her run faster. Cadilla was soon abreast Malla Prasad and was overtaking him.

"Wheee", winnied the mare as the pehelwan on her back fired into the air, "this is terrific".

"Yahooo", neighed the horses, "Charge".

"Eeeeeh", squealed Malla Prasad as he realized that he was losing ground. The gunmen on his back were excitedly firing in the air.

The animals raced to the entrance of the village and were soon dashing down the road to the polling booth when tragedy struck. Bhalua and his men had prepared a trap and were waiting patiently in ambush near the empty polling booth. His men were hidden behind houses or doors and had the stolen 303 rifles and revolvers aimed down the road. They saw the camel race into view closely followed by the horses and the elephant and looked down the cross hairs of their rifles sights.

"Don't shoot until I give the order", ordered the burly bare backed, dark skinned Bhalua who had his rifles cross hairs aimed at the approaching camels chest.

"Don't shoot unless comrade Bhalua orders", ordered the one eyed Jack who had his single eye looking down the cross hairs which were aimed at the approaching Rani. He concentrated on her chest and bobbing head and was not perturbed by the din of the mad gunfire that accompanied the animals.

"Let them come closer", whispered Bhalua as the galloping camels chest grew bigger in his sights.

"Shoot to kill", shouted the one eyed Jack, "but only when comrade Bhalua orders."

Bhalua watched the camel gallop closer then shouted "FIRE", as he pulled the trigger. He felt the thud of the recoil on his shoulder and saw the camel crash neck first onto the ground as dust shot up and the rump shot into the air throwing the two riders over its head who also fell head first to the ground. The camel broke its neck as the body somersaulted and crashed on the gravel as more shots rang out and some horses with their riders came crashing to the ground.

Bhalua pulled and pushed his rifle bolt and looked down the sights at the approaching elephant with the five humans sitting on it. The cross hairs settled on the rider, the mahout. He pulled the trigger and the mahout fell back but remained lying on the elephant with his legs still straddling the latter's neck.

More shots rang out and two gunmen who were sitting on the elephants back toppled to the ground.

The elephant ran on as the remaining men jumped off. They got up and ran to the safety of a house.

Malla Prasad had heard the gunshots when he entered the village and saw Cadilla crash neck first to the ground and somersault on her back, sending Jogi and the gunman flying into the air to fall chest first onto the ground. He saw the horses somersault throwing their riders as they did so. Malla Prasad himself felt multiple stings as bullets thwacked into his thick skin and ricocheted away. The loud cracks of gunfire and the sight of the falling animals frightened him and he stopped, received a few more stings, turned to the right and was soon bulldozing through a thatched house and a little lane which led out of the village. He was lucky the naxalites didn't know how to shoot down an elephant.

Outside in the open he noticed that a few horses with their riders still on their backs were desperately galloping away so he also picked up speed. He knew by the lightness on his back, that the gunmen had either jumped off or had fallen off. What he did not know was that Jehangir had taken a bullet in his head and was lying dead on his back with his legs astride the neck and the feet wedged to the base of his ears.

Running for a couple of kilometres Malla Prasad grew tired and stopped and waited for an order from Jehangir. None came so he stood there and rumbled. "Cadilla, what happened to you? I saw you and Rani fall with the other horses. My god please run out from that village alive. Please Cadilla, please for god's sake come out of that village alive". Malla Prasad was hoping and didn't know that at that moment the camel was lying dead in the middle of the road with a broken neck and a bullet in her heart Rani was on the ground giving faint kicks as her death throes died out, with a few dead or dying humans groaning nearby. One of the pehelwans had a broken neck and further on two riders lay dead and the gunman who had shared Cadilla's hump with Jogi lay moaning on his back on the ground. Jogi had managed to limp off and was now limping desperately through the fields towards Ramnagar and the zemindars mansion. The riders who had miraculously escaped were now desperately galloping back to their village and the naxalites who were jubilant were exhorting the villagers to come out and cast their votes. They did not give chase. They had killed enough and knew that they had broken the enemies back. The remnants of the attacking army had scurried off as a dog sometimes does with its tail between its legs.

Standing for a couple of hours in the middle of the field waiting for his bald masters orders, Malla Prasad noticed something queer. Liquid was slowly trickling down the right side of his right fore leg. He touched the liquid with his trunk. It was red. Dark saffron red. It was blood.

"What happened up there?", thought the elephant, "did a gunman die on my back?". He continued waiting for his masters orders as he stood still for some more time with the blood trickling down. Then he saw the birds. They were flying in round circles above him and were hook beaked vultures.

"Why are you flying over me?", asked the elephant. He could feel his masters legs straddling his neck with the feet stuck to the base of his ears. "What's your problem?"

"There's a dead man on you back", they replied. "His legs are across your neck".

"The man with his legs astride my neck?, do you mean him?".

"Yes, he has a hole in his head".

Malla Prasad was disturbed as suspicious blood shot through his system. "Does he have a bald head?", he asked.

"Yes".

"And a billy goats beard?".

"Yes".

The elephant trumpeted and shook his head. The dead man did not fall off , so the elephant violently shook its head again. He wanted the person to fall off so that he could see for himself.

"The dead man's feet are wedged to your ears", informed the vultures.

Malla Prasad lifted his trunk high up and trumpeted, then lowered it and undid the right ankle from the ear. The violent head shake had tilted the body to the left of the blood soaked mattress. With the leg un-hooked , the body slowly slid down and fell head first to the ground.

Seeing the clothes the elephant swiveled around and squealed. "No, no, please god not him. Of all the people, please not him".

The body was crouched double so the elephant felt with its trunk and pulled at both the feet to straighen it. Turning the body over on its back, he saw the face. It looked red with blood smeared over it and for a moment it seemed as though it wasn't Jehangir but some one else. A ray of hope flickered in the elephants eyes but died when he recognized the billy goat beard and the bald head.

Squealing its grief the huge beast slowly sat down facing the dead man when it remembered. THE LEARNED DOCTOR. The man who had claimed that camels urine was a potent medicine. Giving another squeal he heaved his heavy body up and drew his trunk around the dead man's abdomen. Lifting it up, he headed for Ramnagar and walked through the fields as the crow flies.

"May be the doctor will bring him back to life", he thought. He had watched the bald pig tailed gentleman on many occasions when he had applied various lotions to the various animals so squealing and running cross country with his dead load, Malla Prasad was full of hope. People in the fields all the way to Ramnagar saw the elephant running with a dead human wrapped in its trunk and soon the beast barged into the little village carrying its little load and deposited it gently on the doctors door-step. It was a mud walled room with a thatched roof and contained a table and some chairs and a bench on which injured Jogi was lying.

Hearing the squeal the doctor came out followed by Jogi whom he was treating . He had heard the story from the latter and knew about the disaster. He knelt over the dead body and taking the wrist the felt for the pulse. There was none. He looked into the eyes and shook his head. There was no life in the man, so the doctor got up to go back into his clinic. Something caught hold of his dhoti. Looking around, he realized it was the elephant's trunk. Jogi moved forward and freed the dhoti from the trunk and let the doctor go in. Then taking hold of the trunk he walked forward.

"Come on Malla let's go home", he said.

The elephant did not move but brought back its trunk and twined it around the dead mans abdomen. He then turned around and walked behind Jogi back to the zemindars mansion and his home the Haathikhana.

"The Female Elephant"

Malla Prasad had laid down the dead body in front of the Hathikhana, and sat down behind it with his feet facing the body. He sat the whole night there rambling softly from inside his belly. "Oh lord, may his soul rest in peace , please take his soul to heaven".

"What happened ", whispered the cows.

"Did you ever hear of the charge of the light brigade?," asked headache. He was scared of the elephant so he spoke in whispers.

"No," whispered back the cows.

"Well it was about some foolish men soldier's who charged against ack-ack guns, stinger missiles and sand busters, and were all slaughtered by these mighty weapons."

"What happened to the elephant keeper and the camels and horses".

"What they did a similar charge and the humans called naxalites used AWACK's to monitor their movement. At the precise moment they threw their bows and arrows and picked up stingers and sand busters and blasted their from the face of the earth.

"My god and the elephant came out alive?"

"Well it seems he's made up of different metal".

The cows looked around at the moaning elephant, "Ok how he moan's over his dead keeper," said a short Jersey.

"He was a nice sort of fellow, " replied another cow.

"What nice?" belched the bull.

"Ssh h h h h" shushed the cows, " or Malla might hear."

"Oh yes I forgot", whispered the bull." How could you call a fellow nice when he snatched your hay and gave it to those horses and camels".

"Well there was plenty for everyone".

"Plenty for everyone", whispered the bull, "PLENTY FOR EVERYONE MY FOOT" he belched, "What the hell do you think of the world. There are millions of cows and bulls out there who do not have a roof and die of hunger because of a shortage of hay, and you lazy females say there is plenty of hay, and waste it over those insect like animals.

"Will you shut up", squealed the elephant.

"Oh sorry, sorry, sorry".

The elephant went on slowly moaning and crying as his dead keeper lay in front of him.

"You saw the head", whispered the bull, "It has a hole in it stinger managed to penetrate it.

Jogi limped over to where the elephant sat, closely followed by a pehelwan. "The master is ferocious", he said.

"I know", replied the pehelwan," I'm leaving my job and leaving tonight".

"Why?"

"The police are coming tomorrow to arrest us all".

"But I don't have anywhere to go, moreover the master advised me to tell the police that I wasn't in the fight. I was here tending the animals".

The two man walked over to the dead body.

"Get rid of him," suggested the pehelwan.

"No, the master said that the police would take him

and there will be a post post-mortem, after that he will be buried".

"Who's behind us?"

It was the zemindar who had quietly walked over and was standing behind the two people who had turned around and who namastayed him. "Where is the dead body", the zemindar asked.

The two men pointed towards the elephant, "There master".

The zemindar walked over and stood over the corpse. After saying a silent prayer he knelt down and looked down at the dead face and wept. "Sorry Jehangir, sorry", he apologized through soles. "Thank you for doing all you did for me. Thanking you my friend thank you, I am indebted to you".

"Master please don't weep" Jogi interrupted.

"Will the two of you go and leave me alone".

"Yes master".

"Jehangir you have left me alone in this world to fight the naxalites by myself. One thing I know is you will probably be on your way to heaven. That is the only place for people like you. As for myself, well tomorrow I will be on my way to jail. I have a grouse against you my friend. You left me highly indebted to you. You did not leave anyone in this world to whom I could repay the debt to".

The elephant thought it saw something peculiar from corner of its eyes looked up. A spectator stood behind the sobbing zemindar. The spectator hinted at a bold head and a filly goats beard, and had a kindly face which was looking down at the zemindar. It seemed to telling the zemindar that there was a way of repaying his debt, and that was by being kind to other living creatures especially the ones that were less fortunate than him. "You know master," he seemed to say. "I have entered into the other world and realize that every one here laugh at you living beings. All you, values are wrong you people don't understand life, what you crave and fight for has no meaning. They are just material things which are temporarily with you. They aren't permanently and you have to leave them one day.

The elephant excitedly squealed and got up. The apparition walked over to it and stroked the trunk. "Tell the master," that living is not important but how you live is. What finally counts is how you treat your fellow beings. Then you won't have to fear the naxalites".

Malla Prasad squealed as the apparition vanished. He squealed gain and felt the air where the apparition had stood. There wasn't anything there, and seeing him wave with his trunk Jogi ran over and pulled back the zemindar.

"Why did you do that?"

"Master the elephant nearby hit you."

The zemindar looked at the huge beast and saw its upraised trunk. "I forgot about the elephant," he muttered turned around and wiped the tears from his eyes. "I got carried away by the sight of the dead body. I forgot that the elephant would also be angry with me.

The zemindar walked away as Malla Prasad squealed. "Jogi" the zemindar called the cowherd.

"Yes master".

"Did Jehangir teach you how to look after the elephant. How to control it and deal with it".

"Yes master".

"Then you are in charge of the elephant from today."

"Thank you master".

Early the next morning two police Jeeps entered the courtyard and stopped in front of the mansion. Some policemen entered the verandah while four of them walked past the shed to the Hathikhana. Jehangir's blood dried body had taken a yellowish tinge, gave out a putrid smell and flies buzzed over it. The policemen tied handkerchief over their noses and taking hold of a limb each carried the dead body as the elephant quietly watched. The body was made to lie on the jeeps floor board. Avadesh Prasad was politely handcuffed and led into the other jeep which drew away followed by the second jeep. The fat mistress soon walked out of the verandah as servants piled her belongings into the zemindars jeep. Climbing in, the driver drove her out.

"Now where did she go?", squealed Malla Prasad.

"Don't know", replied the cows.

Malla missed the stallion and the more. They always had ready replies to his questions. Her didn't want the fat mistress to go away. He liked her because of the yellow round balls she gave him to eat whenever she went to pray to him.

The gloomy animal heard the tinkle of the bells and looked up to see four glum human faces lead butter cup back to the cowshed. It seemed like the expected departure of the human soul had departed, and butter cup had done her job of lending the dying man her tail.

"Welcome back my dear Butter," belched, "Welcome back home. How are you, and how is your tail".

"Don't speak of it, I feel filthy. Imagine a dying human holding your tail and then a dead one clasping it. The fingers had to be opened to free my tail Ugh".

"Well it must have been an experience. I waited for you the whole night, anyway did you hear what happened yesterday".

"Yes I did. The humans around the dying man were speaking about it. It was a disaster with the camels, humans and all those horses dead. How sad. Look at Malla there, look how lonely he looks".

"He deserves it", whispered the bull. "I told him not to middle with the mighty humans. I warned him several times, but who listens to a bull. We are regarded as brainless".

Jogi walked over to the elephant and opened the ropes lying the feet. Taking the little spear, and allow he climbed to the head of the elephant and sat with his legs astride the neck. And gong the base of the ears he commanded the elephant. "Agath", he commanded "Agath", and Malla Prasad walked out of the Haathikhana past the cows, through the courtyard and out of the double lioned gates to finally turn left towards the Ganges. Reaching the fifteen acre cane field, Malla Prasad stopped and Jogi climbed down. Taking the dhoti he went to lack at the cane and soon had cut a neat little pile. Shearing the cane off the tall grass, he walked over to the elephant and ordered it to sit down. "Chasing Malla chasing" he ordered. Malla Prasad sat down and Jogi puled the cane onto the huge back. He then took a rope and tied it around the sugar cane and elephant's belly. With the sugar cane firmly on the back, he climbed up the trunk and perched himself on the neck where Jehangir used to sit. Nudging the pachyderm's ears, he "agathed", it forward and headed down the road back to the village. Reaching the intersection, instead of turning left towards the mansion, Jogi pulled the right ear making the elephant turn to the right.

"Now where is he taking me?", thought the elephant as he headed towards the highway. Reaching the tarmaced road the cowshed turned the elephant to the left and headed towards a sleepy little town called Lakhisarai. The elephant soon walked into the bazaar and was surrounded by inquisitive children. Jogi got down and led him to the vegetable market which was made in of two rows of shops attached ruffs and thatched walls. Chaiy Malla chaiy, he ordered the elephant to sit down and living him there he disappeared into a shop and emerged again with the shop keeper who was a short man wearing a pair of green trousers and a check shirt.

"How much do you want for the care?", asked the shopkeeper.

"Four hundred rupees", replied Jogi.

"Its too much".

"How much will you pay?"

"Two hundred rupees".

"Its too little".

"Okay then I will pay two hundred and twenty five".

"I'll take three hundred and nothing less".

"Its final?"

"Yes its final".

"Its a deal".

The shopkeeper handed over the three hundred rupees to Jogi who was opening the ropes. Taking the money and tying it in a little bundled in his dhoti, he opened the ropes and let the care fall. He bent down and helped the shop keeper to collect the care and stack it in the shop. With the last care stacked, he thanked the shopkeeper and climbed on to the elephants neck.

"I think we are going back to the cane field", thought the elephant as it got up.

"Thanks for the cane", shouted the shopkeeper. And when ever you cut some more, bring it to my shop, I will be at your service".

"I will be bringing the cane daily now", replied Jogi. "Previously it used to be fed to this useless animal. That Muslim gentleman was an idiot and used to feed it to this blunderbuss".

The shopkeeper laughed and Jogi" agathed" , Malla Prasad forward. It had downed on the elephant that his new keeper was a thief and had just pilfered his food and sold it. He had taken advantage of the confusion after yesterday's incident. The pehelwan had run away, the zemindar had gone to jail, and the mistress had taken her little child and had gone to live in her city house in the comparative safety of the city of Patna. Jehangir was by now most probably a fairy up there, so there was no one to watch him and complain to the master.

"Agathing" Malla Prasad the two soon left the little town and were walking down the highway. Reaching the spot where they had climbed onto the highway they followed the dirt track which led to the mansion and stopped midway near a huge banyan tree. The elephant was made to stand below some traceless which hung down. Standing on the huge back Jogi took the dhow and hacked at the stems and twigs and little branches that had a cluster of leaves on them. He cut them and stacked them on the back, and when he realized that there was enough, he took the rope and passed it over the banyan greenery stacked on the back, he climbed on the trunk and tied a knot tightly under the belly. Throwing the rope over the greenery to the other side, he collected it and tied another knot. Satisfied that the leaves and branches were firmly on the back, he took hold of the trunk and led it lack to the zemindars mansion and the Hathikhana.

"Does this person think I will eat this", wondered the elephant as he sat on his belly while Jogi unloaded the branches. The bulls and cows were equally surprised at the huge green leap on the elephant's back.

"Is that your food?", asked a cow.

"Don't know", rumbled the elephant, "we have just came back from town. He sold all the sugar cane he had hacked today".

"We always knew he was a thief when ever he got a chance he would quietly milk us and sell the milk in that town".

"What am I going to eat?".

Jogi got down and stacked the leaves and branches in front at the elephant. "There eat", he said.

Malla Prasad looked at him.

"Eat them", Jogi ordered.

"I want my sugar cane", Malla Prasad squealed.

"Eat", ordered Jogi and took a branch which was full of leaves and held it out to the elephant. The elephant did not take it.

Jogi picked up a huge stick and thwacked the fore foot, "now eat this", he ordered.

The elephant did not move so he pushed the branch up and tried to stuff the leaves into the mouth. "Eat", he said.

The elephant turned its head away. So Jogi thwacked the fore feet with his stick again.

"Now he's going too far", commented headache who had been watching the proceedings quietly, "he beating jumbo and jumbo getting irritated and he is an and in front of him. The crunch will soon come.

The crunch came and Malla Prasad snatched the branch from his hand and swinging it at him, hitting him on the back and sending him sprawling to the ground on his stack.

"You deserved that", squealed the elephant as it delivered two more swings at the person who was now terrified and lifting himself had scampered off.

"How does he expect me to eat that", complained Malla Prasad. He unfortunately had to eat it. As night drew on his hunger became unbearable so he slowly extended his trunk and taking a branch he brushed it against his feet, then turned his trunk in a U and put the leaves into his open mouth. Closing the gums he pulled the branch out and it was lifeless. The leaves were in the mouth.

"Hummmm, not bad", thought the elephant, "not bad" no it was on chewing at the leaves and branches the whole night.

The next day Jogi confronted Malla Prasad and uneasily asked him to sit. "Chaiy Malla chaiy", he ordered and to his relief the elephant sat down. He cautiously went to the right of the elephant and climbed on to the neck. He had the spear, the dhow and the rope with him. "Malla Maiy", he ordered and the elephant stood up. "Agath", he ordered and the elephant was lumbering out of the Hathikhana, and out of the double lioned gates on its way to the Ganges and the cane field. reaching it, Jogi hacked at the cane and loaded it on to the elephant back and tied it tightly with a rope. Getting to the back, he "agathed", the elephant back to the Hathikhana and unloaded a part of the sugar cane. Re-tying the rope, he climbed back on to the neck and guided his ward all the way to the little town and the vegetable market where the cane was unloaded and Jogi accepted the money that was paid. It was on the road outside the village that Malla Prasad saw her.

He saw an elephant in the distance and his heart leapt. It was coming his way so when the cane closer, he gave her a "hello".

"Hello", she replied.

There was a mattress on her back and a man with a spear and a shotgun was sitting and straddling her neck, with four dhoti and kurta clad people behind him.

"Are you a male or female"

"Female"

Malla Prasad was smitten with love, his eyes twinkled and had the female elephant was embedded in them. It was a love at first sight. "You look lovely" he said.

"You look smart".

"You look beautiful".

"You look handsome".

"I like you".

"I love you too".

Sizzling what was happening the two mahouts started Jabbing at the heads of their different wards with their spears and kicked into their huge ears to agath them on.

"These humans are a nuisance", rumbled Malla Prasad.

"Yes they are".

"Then lets get rid of them".

"I can't I respect him".

"I don't respect mine, he just sold a stomach full of sugar cane just now".

Obeying her masters Agath, the female walked on. "Think I'll have to say good bye", she rumbled.

"No don't, squealed Malla Prasad.

Jogi went on jumbling his spear at the head and pulled at the left ear.

"No squealed Malla Prasad as he swing his trunk over his head and spent Jogi toppling to the ground. The latter banged his head on the hard tarmac. Turning around and giving another squealed Malla Prasad ran back and having his fore feet up he tried to bring it over her back but missed.

"Watch out", shouted the men on the female elephants back "that elephant has gone mad".

Jabbing the spear into the females head, her mahout agathed her to move fast. The elephant responded and was soon running.

"Stop my dear stop", squealed Malla Prasad as he himself picked up speed and caught up with her. He suddenly turned to the left and heaved his fore feet up. His knee hit a couple of people and sent then trembling down from the mattress. The terrified humans picked themselves up and scampered off across the wheat fields.

"Stand still my dear", Malla Prasad squealed as he rubbed the side of his face against the female belly. "You do feel nice my dear. You do feel nice".

The two remaining humans left sitting on the female elephants mattress kicked at Malla Prasad's head. "Yah, go, go, go yah, yah", they shouted and jumped óff the back to avoid the elephants trunk which was swing at them. From the ground they shouted to the mahout to shoot in the air. Malla Prasad was now nuzzling the female just below the mattress as the mahout hastily loaded his shot gun and fired in the air.

"What was that", squealed the elephant as it heard all sorts of noises in its ears. The blast from the gun had half deferred it. "I can't hear, What happened?"

The mahout pulled the second trigger and the blast sent more sparrowy noises twittering into Malla Prasad's ears.

"My god, he's using a fire stick", Malla Prasad squealed and pulled away. Turning around he did not even say a good bye to the pretty looking female and squealed and ran all the way back to the safety of his Hathikhana.

Seeing him running in head ache got a fright and scampered out of the way. "What was that", he belched. "Jumbo's running as though a dragon's chasing him". Then looking towards the courtyard, he realized that no one was chasing the elephant.

"That's queer", the bull commented", no one's chasing him".

Malla Prasad had reached the Hathikhana and was

looking around for Jogi.

"What scared you Jumbo?"

"It was a fire stick".

"A fire stick?"

"Yes a fire stick, and do you know something, today I realized that a female part of me existed".

"Hey don't tell me your on head again?"

"Shut up will you, I saw a female elephant today. An elephant just like me with a trunk, a tail and tusks."

"And huge falarial feet?"

"Shut up, but yes she had feet like mine".

"Then why didn't you take her".

"Her master aimed his firesticks at me, so I had to run away".

"Was it a stringer or a scud?"

"Will you shut up, I hate these humans. I hate these humans I hate them with all my heart. Today I realized that they purposely kept me away from a spouse all my life. These humans are our masters and we are their slower to be mistreated and maltreated by them. They did not have the right to keep me away from my own world, from the animals of my own kind. I hate these humans. I hate these humans, Oh how I hate these humans, I wish I could kill all of them.

Death To The Elephant

Day's passed and Malla Prasad got used to the sight of Jogi stealing the sugar cane which was supposed to be fed to him.

He did not like Jogi as much as he liked the bald Jehangir and he missed the Muslim gentleman. Of course he had his usual grouse.

He wanted a spouse which Jogi or the manager refused to give him. The zemindar was still appealing to the courts for bail so he sent munsif Mahavir Lal back to the mansion to handle his affairs. Jogi was a thief. The bespectacled manager who always had a notepad in his hand, proved to be a bigger one. The fat mistress had refused to come back to the mansion. She felt that rural Bihar had become too dangerous to live in and stayed back in the comparative safety of urban Patna. The result was that Jogi and the manager had a field day. Jogi was not disturbed when he sold the milk stolen from the udders of Avadesh's cows and the cane from Malla Prasad's cane field. He in turn turned a blind eye when the manager stole half of the harvest and sent it to his own home and the other half to the master's city residence in Patna. The manager in fact took a cut from Jogi as his share of the stolen milk.

"What's happened to our hay?", moaned Buttercup.

"The manager sells off most of the hay after the harvest and leaves only a bare minimum for us", complained Headache.

The news reached Avadesh Prasad in jail who was exasperated. He knew that his wife would refuse to go back to the mansion. He himself had decided to live in Patna after he was released from jail, so he ordered Mahavir Lal to sell off all his bovines, which the latter gleefully did. He sold the cows for ten thousand rupees a piece, pocketed four thousand and sent the rest six thousand to the mistress in Patna. Soon only half of the cowsheds residents remained.

"I hate these humans", commented Headache," they sold off half my harem. My dear Buttercup was taken away".

"I never liked these humans", commented Neckache as he also had lost half of his harem.

"I wish the master came back from the city", mooed a cow.

"I heard the humans speak", continued Headache," the master and mistress won't be coming back".

"The manager and Jogi will make us die of hunger", commented a hornless Jersey cow. "What do we do now ?"

"Swat them on their bottoms", squealed Malla Prasad.

The cows turned and poked their heads out of the cowshed. "But we don't have a trunk like yours", they replied.

"Yes, but you have horns, you can make two huge holes in their bottoms".

"Look here Jumbo, I know you're hot headed and I also know you are foolish", belched Headache. "How do you expect us to fight the humans ?".

"Ram them".

"But they have AWAC's

"Kick them",

"But they have Spitfires, and Hurricanes and Jaguars and F16's".

"Horn them".

But they have Bazooka's, and, ack-ack's and Harpoons and Shermans and Patons and Tigers and anti tank guns.

"KILL THEM".

"But they have the atom bomb, the nitrogen bomb and the hydrogen bomb".

"Then go to hell".

"Thank you, but to remind you once more, we are not as hot headed as you. We know the human's well and know how profitable IT is not to meddle with them. We had in fact advised you not to meddle with them. But you and your friends did not listen to our advice and what was the result? You are the only ones alive here.

The rest are playing on the harp somewhere up there".

"Or guitaring in hell", added Neckache.

"You are all cowards", rumbled Malla Prasad. "Cowards who aren't fit to be called animals. I hate the humans and have slammed their rumps like this. "The elephant's trunk swung down in a mock attack." And this and in future when ever I get a chance, I will go on swatting them".

"Then you'll kill yourself Jumbo, you'll kill yourself", replied Headache.

"I won't die, I was born to live, and I will l live, and when ever I get a chance to swat them , I will take it".

"Have your way Jumbo. Everyone is master of his

own life".

"I am the master of my own life".

"Don't squander it".

"Sh-Sh", shushed a cow." I think I can hear an iron horse approaching".

The cow was right. A red jeep drew up in the courtyard and an elderly tall white haired gentleman climbed out. "I would like to meet the manager of this place," he asked .

Mahavir Lal walked upto him with his hands folded in a namastay. "Yes what is it?"

"I hear you are in charge of an elephant?"

"Yes".

"I would like to rent it for two days . On the fifteenth of this month is my son's wedding and I have rented five more elephants for the baraat. I could pay you three thousand rupees for both the days".

"You have forgotten to introduce yourself?", reminded the manager.

"Sorry, I forgot. By profession I am a contractor in the railways and I live in Birbigha, anything else you want to know?"

"Give us your address sir", replied Mahavir Lal. "We will discuss your offer with the master, and then well inform you".

The contractor pulled out a wallet from his kurta pocket and opening it he pulled out a card and handed it over to the manager. "Here take this, but remember there are only six days left and I'd like your answer as soon as possible".

The three humans namastayed each other and the contractor climbed into the Jeep. "Please send me your answer as soon as possible", he reminded as his Jeep pulled away.

"Now what do you think of the offer?", Mahavir Lal asked Jogi.

"Nice".

"Two thousand for me and one thousand for you".

"No, fifteen hundred for both of us", replied Jogi.

"Then I won't agree. I won't allow the elephant to go".

Jogi's grin disappeared as he understood the manager' sterms. "Agreed? Or not Jogi?", asked Mahavir Lal.

"Agreed, but this is not fair".

"Okay I'm writing a letter to this gentleman. You will take it and deliver it to him and don't forget to bring back an advance of a thousand rupees".

The manager walked off to write the letter and Jogi walked upto Malla Prasad. He stroked the trunk and looked up at the huge head. "So Malla, you are going to be our milch cow now", he said.

' It seems like you will earn us a lot of money".

"I want a wife", Malla Prasad rumbled.

"Mahavir Lal and I will be letting you on hire soon",

"Look Jogi, I saw the female elephant, and I want her".

"You are going to make us rich", Jogi turned around and bent down to lift some leaves to give the elephant to eat when the trunk moved back and shot forward, connecting the cow-herd's

bottom and the man was sent crashing head first to the ground".

"How did you like that for a starter?", squealed Malla Prasad.

"You'll get yourself killed", belched Headache,

"you're stubborn, you refuse to learn".

Days passed and six more cows were sold and Jogi came back from the contractors village with the one thousand rupees in advance money. He pocketed five hundred and gave the other five to the manager.

"Go take the elephant", the manager ordered.

Jogi cautiously approached the elephant and ordered it to sit. " Chaiy Malla chaiy", he said and was relieved when the elephant sat down, so he fetch the little spear and rope and hanging the bells around the neck, he climbed onto the back and sat down with his feet straddling the neck.

"Maiy Malla Maiy", he ordered and the elephant got up. Nudging the base of the huge ears with his feet, he ordered the elephant to move forward.

"Agath", he ordered, "Agath", and poked the spear lightly on

the head.

Malla Prasad walked out of the Hathikhana, looking majestic and as usual the cows drooled over him.

"He's handsome".

"He's smart".

"He's Macho".

"Shut up", belched the bulls. "And put your heads back in".

Malla Prasad was walking easily as he swayed gently to right and to the left. He did not hurry and it seemed like Jogi was enjoying the walk as he didn't hurry him on.

"I hope I see that girl today", rumbled the elephant, but was unfortunate. He did not see the girl elephant on the way to the sleepy little town where Jogi used to sell his sugar cane. He did not see the girl elephant all the way to the railway line . He crossed the line and did not see the girl elephant all the way to Birbigha and the bride grooms house where he saw five male elephants like himself.

"Hello", greeted a huge tusker.

"Hello", replied Malla Prasad.

"Hello", greeted the other elephants.

"Hello", replied Malla.

"What's your name?", asked the tusker.

"Malla Prasad".

"I'm Gajanand Prasad".

"And I'm Paddum Prasad".

"And the rest?", asked Malla.

"Well he's, Daku Prasad and he's Pachim Prasad and he's Fateh Prasad and that there is Amiri Prasad".

"Glad to meet you all", replied Malla, "but tell me are you male or a female?"

"We are all males" the tusker replied.

"Have you seen a girl elephant around here".

"No".

"Do any of you have a spouse".

The elephants shook their heads. "No", they all rumbled. "We are all bachelors".

"So am I".

The elephants were standing in a row in a field outside the bridegrooms boundary wall which also had a pair of cement lion's guarding the gates.

"What do you gentlemen think of the humans?", asked Malla Prasad.

"Unpredictable".

"They pray to me", continued Malla.

" To me also".

"And to me"

"And to me"

"They feed me leaves of the peepal and mango tree", continued Malla.

"And me"

"And me also".

"They feed the bitter things to all of us", grumbled the tusker.

"You know, there should be a revolution", stated an elephant who was standing in the end of the line "An elephant revolution to free ourselves from the humans".

"That's impossible", replied the tusker, "The humans may look small compared to us. But they have brain's and machines and could easily slaughter the likes of us if they wanted to".

"Then do we continue to live as slaves?".

"Yes, that's if you want to live".

"You speak like the bull who lives near me, back in my home", commented Malla Prasad.

"The bull is wise".

Jogi climbed down the trunk and went and sat with a group of mahouts who were huddled together discussing something or the other.

"How's your mahout?", asked the tusker.

"He's a brat and a thief".

"Mine is a gentleman ".

"I had a gentleman once".

A jeep roared over to the doubled lioned gate but was stopped by a man who was standing in the middle of the gate who had a raised hand. Malla Prasad recognized the man as the one who had come in the red iron horse and had talked with the manager. He did not recognize the who had came out of the jeep with folded hands. They all had yellow turbans on their heads and wore yellow dhoti's and white kurtas.

"Please don't be stubborn sir," requested a man who had his hands folded.

"Nothing doing", replied the contractor who was still blocking

the entrance gate. "I have showed you enough patience".

"But please sir".

"No I will not accept".

One of the men with folded hands walked over to the contractor and opened his turban and put it on the latter' s feet. "Please accept this", he requested.

"No I want money", replied the contractor.

"Why are they wearing yellow clothes?", asked Malla Prasad. "They are all wearing yellow".

"Yellow is an auspicious colour for the Hindu's", replied the tusker, "that's why it is used during marriages".

"They seem to be quarrelling", commented Malla Prasad as he watched the contractor flail his hands and motion towards the road that led to his gates.

"He's telling those people to go back", commented the tusker.

"Why?".

"Oh its the usual, I've seen it happen in most of the marriages I've attended. They are squabbling over money".

"Over money?"

"Yes over dowry money".

"It seems this new comer doesn't understand", rumbled the elephant who was standing in the end of the line. "IS this your first experience of a human marriage?"

"Yes" replied Malla.

"No wonder, any way I'll tell you", continued the tusker. "When a human marries his daughter, he has to pay some money as a dowry to the male human's parents. He sometimes is unable to pay, and a row takes place".

"That's weird", replied Malla Prasad.

The shouting and hand flailing continued on both sides and suddenly all the people who were wearing yellow dhoti's lay flat

on the ground.

"Now why did they do that?", asked Malla Prasad.

"Go on looking, the climax is coming" replied the tusker.

The contractor shouted and some men came running from the mansion. One of them handed the tall gentleman a shotgun. He took the weapon and fired two shots in the air and turned around to go but stopped as the yellow dhotied people suddenly got up and one of the mpokedh is head into the jeep and came out holding a suit case. Holding it up, he walked upto the contractor and opened it and showed the insides to him.

"Aaah", the contractor's mouth opened in a smile as he shut the suit case and took it and handed it to one of his men, after which the yellow dhotied men who were now all smiling took turns to bear hug. The smiling gentlemen were now all twirling their moustache's with their right hands as though something important had been settled.

"What happened?", asked Malla Prasad.

"The yellow dhotied humans are the brides family",

explained the tusker, "and they come to request the bride groom's father to forgive them a certain amount of the dowry money. The bridegroom's father refused so the bride's family prostrated themselves on the ground before him, begged. He refused and pointed to the road telling them to go away, that the marriage was cancelled. To show that he was angry, he fired two shots in the air and then turned to walk away. This was the signal that the crunch had come so the bride's family got up and took out the suitcase which was full of money and gave it to him, and the problem was solved".

"You mean to say they had the money all along?"

"Yes".

"Then why did they beg?"

"They made a last ditch attempt to reduce the dowry amount. They were unsuccessful so they sportingly accepted the defeat".

" Weird, weird, weird", Malla shook his head, "I wish the bulls were here to witness this". Then turning to the tusker he asked "Don't you want a wife, a spouse, a female elephant?".

"Of course I do?"

Malla turned to the other elephants. "Don't you all want a wife?"

"Yes we all do".

"You know, I saw a girl elephant a few day's ago. I wanted to talk to her but the humans fired their fire sticks at me".

"I've never seen a female in my life", commented the tusker, "How was she?"

"Beautiful, gorgeous".

Malla Prasad had attracted the attention of all the

elephants. "Did she have a trunk?", asked the tusker.

"Yes".

"How was it"

"Perfect".

"Ooooooh", the elephants drooled.

"Did she have a tail?"

"Yes".

"How was it?"

"Beautiful".

"Ooooh".

"And feet like ours".

"Yes".

"How were they?"

"Streamlined and silky".

"Ooooh".

"How did you know she was a female?", asked another elephant.

"She told me so, and she smiled at me and I nearly vomited my heart out in excitement".

"Is that how you feel when you first see a female?", asked the tusker.

"Yes".

A frown crossed the elephant's face. One thing he was sure was that he didn't want to vomit his heart out. He loved his heart and wanted it to stay where it usually stayed. Inside his huge body.

"Here come our mahouts", interrupted another elephant as the mahouts walked over to their wards and took hold of their trunks. Except for Jogi, the rest were Muslim gentlemen and wore kurta's over lungies of assorted colours. Some were fat while others were of medium build. Some of them had huge whiskers while the man holding the tusker's trunk had a billy goats beard on his chin just like Jehangir's. All of them were dark in complexion.

The mahouts led their wards to the double lioned gate in a line. The yellow dhotied humans had got into their jeep and had driven off to the brides house.

"Now What's going to happen?", asked Malla Prasad.

"Plenty, just keep quite and keep on watching", replied the tusker.

There was a loud noise inside the double lioned gate. It was the brass band which had come into action. They blasted the stillness of the Behari evening with their trumpets, horns and drums, and disturbed the sound waves that entered the elephant's ears.

"What a ruckus they are making", commented an elephant.

"They call it music and dance to its tune," answered the tusker.

The band slowly walked out of the double lioned gate with some men in white dhoti's and kurta's dancing and leading the way. Behind the band crawled an open red jeep in which the bridegroom sat next to the yellow turbaned driver. Behind the red jeep crawled a line of assorted cars. Some were ambassadors, Fiats, and Jeeps, and they all had coloured paper stuck to their fenders and grooves in their body work.

"Make the elephants walk behind the red jeep", some one ordered and the mahouts "agathed", their wards forward and lined them up behind the red vehicle.

People were bursting fire crackers while others lifted their gun barrels skywards and fired.

"What a din they are making", commented Malla Prasad who did not like the sound of gunfire. It sounded just like the one in the tiny sudra village where Cadilla and Rani had gone crashing to the ground in a cloud of dust, and his dear Jehangir had died. "I don't like the noise", he grumbled.

"Neither do we", stated the tusker.

"The noise is dangerous, they are using firesticks".

"Shut up and quietly walk," interfered another elephant.

The little cavalcade was passing along a dirt track which passed through a village. Both the sides of the road was packed with people passed funny comments at the animals.

"I don't like these humans", rumbled Malla Prasad.

"Look how they make fun of us", squealed another elephant.

"Look at that fellow making faces at me", rumbled the tusker.

"Look at that person. He's making dirty signs at me".

A villager picked up a stone and threw it at Malla Prasad. It hit the elephant on the head causing it to turn, fall out of line and run towards the stone thrower with an uplifted trunk. The stone thrower and those near him scampered off into the lanes and by lanes of the village.

"I hate these humans", squealed Malla Prasad as Jogi agathed him back in line. A man walked upto the mahout and asked him about his ward. "Is he mad?, Is he dangerous?".

"No sir", replied Jogi. "Those boys threw stones at

the elephant, that's why he reacted angrily".

The person understood and nodded his head and walked on after giving Jogi a warning. "What ever it is, keep a tight control over your ward" he said. "The bridegrooms car is just before you. Nothing untoward should happen".

"Nothing will happen sir". Jogi promised as he held tightly to Malla Prasad's trunk as he led him on.

"I hate these humans", rumbled Malla Prasad, "I hate these humans".

"Cool it friend", warned the tusker, " We are just behind the bride grooms car, and if he gets hurt, all hell will break loose".

"But I hate the humans", continued Malla Prasad, "they killed Jehangir, and refuse me a spouse. Look at that lout in that iron horse. Look at his face. His eyes gleam at the thought of meeting his spouse today".

"Cool it friend cool it", rumbled another elephant.

"I won't", squealed Malla Prasad, " look at the gleam in that humans eyes".

"Watch out, he is the bridegroom," warned another elephant. "Don't touch him".

The little procession soon left the village behind and the elephants were ordered to move on ahead and wait at the brides house to receive the baraat. Jogi "agathed", Malla Prasad as the other mahouts " agathed ", their wards. They all climbed up the trunks and sat themselves on the backs with their legs astride the necks and nudged the base of the ears to make their wards move faster.

They were soon on the highway that led to Patna. Heading north, after two kilometres the road curved in a U and headed south west towards the brides village. After travelling two kilometres southwards, the six elephants left the highway and followed a dirt track which led to the village where they were made to stand in a line in front of the gate of the brides boundary wall.

"Now what will happen?", asked Malla Prasad.

"Well have to wait till the baraat arrives", commented the tusker.

"You know a long time a ago when I was a little child and had been taken to the Sonepur fair to be sold, I swatted a wasp. He turned out to be a learned fellow and said that we elephants were the slaves of the humans".

"The wasp was wise", commented the tusker.

"At that time I thought it was just irritating me. How true his words turned out to be".

"Now look here you fellow", warned the tusker, "it seems you are getting worked up?".

The tusker did not like the change of Malla Prasad's tone.

"I hate these humans", continued Malla Prasad, "they have made us their slaves and refuse us a spouse".

"Shut up and be quite", ordered the tusker.

"I won't",

"This fellow will get us killed ", grumbled the other elephants, but fell silent as the faint sound of drums and trumpets floated to them.

"Now keep quite", ordered the tusker. Not understanding the squeals and rumbles that the elephants were exchanging, Jogi asked a mahout to keep an eye on his ward and walked to a nearby bench spot where he lay down and went to sleep. He knew he had plenty of time since several rituals would be conducted after the Baraat's arrival after which he would be free to take his ward back home.

While Jogi slept, the noisy Baraat came into view and was led by a bunch of highly sozzled dancing revellers. They had drunk a cheap local drink called Mahua which could be compared to the vodka in its ability to blow the brain. Leading the group of drunks was the chief guest. He was the bridegroom's brother in law, his sister's husband and this important positions made the rowdy gentleman rowdier still. He was thin, tall, fair with curly hair on his hand and an improperly tucked dhoti, a part of which dragged on the ground. He was thoroughly enjoying himself as he shook his torso and jiggled his bottom in what was supposed to be a dance and had a packet of "Charminar" cigarette's in one hand and a bottle of hooch in the other.

"What are they doing", asked Malla Prasad as he walked four steps forward and was now blocking the road that led to the brides house.

"Get back", rumbled an elephant "You've fallen out of line".

"I want to see What's happening", replied Malla Prasad.

"Get back".

"Remove the elephant from the road", shouted the band master as he waved to his men to stop.

"Remove the elephant ", shouted a trumpeter.

"Who allowed that elephant to come out of line?"

"Who's incharge of that elephant?"

"Where is the mahout"?

"Remove the blockade as soon as possible".

A mahout took hold of Malla Prasad's trunk and tried to move him back into line. "Pichoo hut", he ordered, "pichoo hut", but Malla Prasad did not budge.

"Pichoo hut", the mahout ordered again," pichoo hut", but Malla Prasad did not move.

"Who does this elephant belong to?", asked the bride groom's father.

"It belongs to Avadesh Prasad of Ramnagar".

"Make it move back?"

"I can't"

"Where is the mahout?"

"He is sleeping there".

"Then wake him".

This was too much for the bridegrooms brother in law. The tall drunk impatient gentleman hardly managed to stand straight so swaying slightly he staggered towards the elephant. "I'll remove the idiot ", he slurred and moved forward while another part of his improperly tucked dhoti fell open and dragged on the ground. Reaching the elephant he stopped and swaying a little , he looked up and through his hooch sozzled eyes he saw the blurred figure of the elephants huge head. He infact saw three elephant's heads with three sets of tusks intermingled with each other.

"Go back", rumbled Malla Prasad.

"Watch it, don't touch that fellow", warned the tusker.

Don't touch him you idiot", warned another elephant.

"I won't", rumbled Malla Prasad.

"This idiot is talking to me", slurred the drunk. "I'll turn it around". He threw the cigarette box and with the empty hand he felt for the tusks and making contact he took hold of it and pulled to turn the head. He was unsuccessful so he tried again as he gave a bigger tug.

"Look what he's doing", squealed Malla Prasad.

"Don't touch that human", warned the tusker. "Let him do what he wants".

"We warn you not to touch him", rumbled the other elephant.

"Okay I won't".

The drunk had finished tugging at the tusk and angry at being unsuccessful , he took a step back and looked up at the three sets of heads.

"Push off you Lilliputian", rumbled Malla Prasad, "I don't like you".

The drunk lifted the hooch bottle and aimed it at the three heads and chose the one that he thought was real. He cursed and threw the bottle which bounced off the head.

This was enough provocation for the elephant.

"You lily livered idiot", squealed Malla Prasad, "you idiotic human, you slave trader, you useless master, you think you can hurt me and get away with it?"

"Watch out", squealed the tusker as Malla Prasad stepped forward and wrapped the drunk in his trunk.

"Let go", squealed another elephant, "My god, don't do it".

Malla Prasad lifted the drunk seven feet up and dashed the body on the ground." This will teach you to hit me", he squealed.

"Let him go, you idiot", trumpeted the tusker, "let him go, you nearly killed him".

"I'll kill him", squealed Malla Prasad as he knelt

down and with his knees he squashed the mans calves. The man was already unconscious and did not move so the elephant brought its tusks in line with the drunks belly. " Now just watch the stomach open", he rumbled.

Malla Prasad pressed the tusk deep into the flesh and the pain brought the man to his senses causing him to scream. "Scream more", squealed the elephant as his head moved up and sent the tusk tearing through the abdomen to crash into the rib cage and enter the chest while the other tusk scraped the ground beside the body.

"My god he did it", squealed an elephant, "lets get out of here before the humans react".

Malla Prasad drew his head down causing the tusk to travel out of the rib cage back into the abdomen while the other tusk re-scraped the ground.

"Lets get out of here", squealed the tusker who wanted to run but was stopped by his mahout who had climbed onto him and was poking his head with his spear to control him. "The idiot will get as all killed", he rumbled.

Malla Prasad did two more up and down movements with his head and satisfied he squealed and got up with a bloody right tusk. "I did it , I killed a human , he squealed, "I've killed a human. I am the king, I'm not a slave any more".

"He's gone mad, by god he's gone mad", squealed another elephant. "Where is his mahout?"

A couple of mahouts had run over to the sleeping Jogi and had woken him. He got up in time to see Malla Prasad get up with a bloody right tusk and trumpet his challenge. As he ran towards his ward, he saw the shocked baraat scamper off in different directions. The terrified bridegroom was the first to run. He jumped out of the red jeep and ran as the door's of the other vehicles flew open and emptied their occupants who fled into the darkness of the adjoining fields.

"Malla Prasad Maiy", ordered Jogi as he ran towards the elephant.

"Take your elephant and run", shouted a mahout", "or they will kill it".

"Run into the fields towards the right", shouted another mahout, "and get out before they can re-group".

Jogi caught hold of Malla Prasad's trunk and turned him around. Leading the Pachyderm into the dark fields he was soon running with the elephant lumbering beside him. "Agath", he shouted, "Agath".

"I killed a human", squealed the elephant, "I killed a human".

Jogi jumped and catching hold of the running elephants trunk he climbed and seated himself behind the bobbing head. "Run Malla", he screamed. "Agath", and kicked the elephant behind the ear.

The elephant picked up speed "Agath Malla", Jogi went on screaming as he violently jabbed the spear into the head and kicked again behind the ear.

The elephant was soon dashing through the paddy fields towards the tarmaced road. Reaching the highway Jogi turned him towards the north west, and jabbing into the head and kicking behind the ears, he coerced the elephant to run on.

"I don't want to run", squealed Malla Prasad, "I

want to fight".

Back in the village the Baraat re-assembled in a nearby Paddy field. "Where are the guns", shouted the bridegrooms father, as a dozen gunmen ran upto him. They all held twelve bore shotguns in their hands. "Lets go back to the village and see if my son in law is alive", he ordered.

The baraat marched back to the village and approached the lifeless figure which lay on the blood soaked ground near the five remaining elephants. The bride's father was standing nearly while his family doctor knelt beside the still figure.

"Is he dead doctor?" asked the bridegroom's father.

"Yes".

"Aaagh", screamed the tall gentleman, "Aayah, my daughter is now a widow."

Some of the revelers ran up to console him but he brushed them away. "All these years I have earned money", he screamed, "I paid five lakh rupees for my daughter's dowry only to see with my own eyes her husband being gored to death by an elephant, Aayah".

The bridegroom ran upto his father but was also brushed aside. "Son", he screamed, "did you see how your brother in law died?"

"Yes father".

"Then Take your revenge".

"How father?"

"SHOOT THE ELEPHANT'S. SHOOT THOSE DARNED ELEPHANTS".

The bridegroom turned around and shouted for the gunmen who came running to him. "Shoot those elephants", he ordered. "Kill them".

The gunmen turned around and loaded their

weapons with two red bullets each and aimed then at the heads of the elephants.

"Nooooo", squealed the tusker, "I am innocent".

"Aeeeee", squealed another elephant, "we did not do it". The mahouts jumped off the heads and ran forward and fell at the gun men's feet." Don't shoot", they pleaded, "these elephants are innocent. The killer has run away."

"Shoot", ordered the bridegroom's father. "Shoot, damn it, shoot".

The tusker's mahout ran upto him and fell at his feet. "You invited us sir ",

he pleaded, "Don't shoot our animals. We are your guests, you cannot harm us, shoot the killer".

"Where is the killer?"

"He and his mahout ran off to the right into those fields. They must have reached the highway by now".

"Where will they be heading?"

"To Ramnagar sir".

The bride's father got exited. "Let these elephants be", he shouted, "bring the jeep over," then turning to the bridegroom's father he asked. " The elephant is running back to Ramnagar is it?"

"Yes".

"The road to Ramnagar travels two kilometres north west, then does a U turn and travels south to your village".

"Yes".

"Then the elephant is running back to your village. We can take a short cut through the fields, go to your village, intercept the killer near there and shoot it".

"Yes that's it", cried the bridegroom's father. "Let these elephants be and bring the jeep. Eight of you with guns, go back to our village and shoot the elephant.

An open jeep roared up as shouts of "Hathi ko Maro", echoed and eight gunmen jumped into the vehicle. "Remember", yelled

the bride groom," we want the elephant dead".

The jeep roared off to the east of the village and ploughed through the paddy fields as it jumped skipped, bucked and bounced over the uneven ground, causing the headlight beam to do a unique jig. The occupants knew that the elephant had taken the wrong route and would now be most probably negotiating the U turn They would dash across the fields and reach the road south of the U turn where they would wait in ambush.

"Agath", screamed Jogi as he violently kicked behind the ear. "Come on Malla run faster", he goaded as he jabbed at the head with the spear. Sitting behind the head he saw to his left the distant headlights of the Jeep bobbing as it raced madly across the uneven fields. He knew the chase was on, so he kicked into the ear base screaming as he desperately jabbed with the spear "I feel like killing you too", squealed the elephant as its trunk shot up in an attempt to hit the mahout.

"Agath", screamed Jogi, "Agath, agath, agath".

Malla Prasad increased his speed as the frightened kicking Jogi watched the bobbing headlights. "Agath", he shouted again as he kicked behind the ears. He was scared now, terrified for his own life, and in his terror he did not realize that if he left the road the elephant would easily outrun the jeep across in the uneven fields. The only thing he could think of now was to make Malla Prasad run faster.

"Drive faster", shouted a gun man as the jeep bucked and bounced over obstacles. Lifting his gun, the excited fellow fired in the air.

Jogi heard the gun shot and realized that the jeeps lights were travelling parallel to the elephant. The vehicle soon left the pachyderm behind and the mahout could see the reddish hue of the little red tail lights in the distance. He got a surprise when the bobbing headlight beam suddenly shot up into the night sky, swung down again and swiveled around with the beam now crossing the elephants path. He got another shock as he realized to his horror that the road had turned in a U and Malla Prasad was now running wildly towards the jeep which had its head lights switched off.

The jeep had lurched as the driver accelerated the vehicle up the incline to the tarmaced road. The headlight beam had shot into the night sky and swung down as the vehicle levelled itself on the road and swiveled to the right as the vehicle followed suite. The lights were now facing the fast approaching elephant so the driver switched them off as the gunmen took their positions and aimed at the silhouette surging towards them.

"Stop", screamed Jogi as he pulled back at the ears. "Stop

Malla stop, Pichoo Hut".

"I won't," squealed the elephant as it ran on, "I want to fight, I want to kill more humans".

"Stop", screamed Jogi as he braced his feet against the ear base and pulled back at the ears. "STOP, RUK".

"Get off my back you coward if you don't want to fight", squealed Malla Prasad as he swung his trunk in a vicious circle which hit Jogi making the mahout fall back.

Jogi got up and received another shot which sent him rolling backwards across the elephants back. He lost his balance and rolled down sideways and fell to the ground.

"Serves you right", squealed the elephant and lifting up its trunk it trumpeted its challenge as it charged on. It had reached a distance of a hundred and twenty feet from the jeep when the driver flicked the head lights on. The gunmen saw the animal was mahoutless, so they aimed with ease not fearing to hit the human. They made minor adjustments to their aim and fired and saw the bullets slam into the pachyderm's head.

The elephant was blown senseless but kept on running. The velocity of the hurtling body refused to stop and the pachyderm ran as though the shots hadn't affected it. The strong legs refused to crumble.

The gunmen fired the second barrels and saw the bullets slam into the bobbing forehead. The hot round balls mashed the senseless brain but the elephant barged on as its hurtling body refused to stop. It seemed as though the monolith refused to be pulled down. "Reverse", screamed a gunman as the panicked driver slammed the gear forward. "Reverse fast", he shouted.

The elephant was now fifty feet from the jeep and in the glare of the headlights it seemed as though the charging monster would run it down, so the driver let go off the clutch and rammed his foot on the accelerator causing the jeep to shoot back as the occupants desperately re-loaded. This was however unnecessary because the elephants head drooped as the right leg gave way. The left leg followed suite and the head and the trunk plunged into the tarmac. The velocity of the hurtling body lifted the buttocks and hind legs a little into the air and for an instant it seemed as though the animal would somersault over its own head. For a split second the body stood still with the forelegs, trunk and head stuck to the tarmac and the posterior with the hind legs slightly in the air. The body slowly turned and with a loud whump fell sideways on the ground and lay still as though the elephant was asleep.

Malla Prasad had met a violent death and was no. Searching for his friends Glaxo, Brufen, Ranbaxy and Cadilla in the happy hunting grounds where he complained.

"My dear friends those humans were bad, a wife, the enjoyment, due to them I never had, You see my friends, I have the same old grouse, they never supplied me with a beautiful spouse."